VOLUME 23

REPUBLIC
P-47 THUNDERBOLT

By Frederick A. Johnsen

Copyright © 1999 Frederick A. Johnsen

Published by
Specialty Press Publishers and Wholesalers
11605 Kost Dam Road
North Branch, MN 55056
United States of America
(612) 583-3239

Distributed in the UK and Europe by
Airlife Publishing Ltd.
101 Longden Road
Shrewsbury
SY3 9EB
England

ISBN 1-58007-018-3

All rights reserved. No part of this book may be reproduced or transmitted in any form or by any means, electronic or mechanical including photocopying, recording or by any information storage and retrieval system, without permission from the Publisher in writing.

Material contained in this book is intended for historical and entertainment value only, and is not to be construed as usable for aircraft or component restoration, maintenance, or use.

Designed by Dennis R. Jenkins

Printed in the United States of America

Front Cover: Open ammunition hatch on wing shows color of zinc chromate primer used on P-47D 42-28688. Guns have been removed for servicing as fueling is accomplished. Some 56th Fighter Group P-47Ds received variegated green and gray camouflage after reaching England. (Brown/USAFA)

Back Cover (left): Incredible views of distorted P-47D horizontal stabilizer show collateral battle damage pock marks on vertical fin as well. (AAF)

Back Cover (top right): A flying pink elephant adorned "Moki" of the 318th Fighter Group. Cuffed Curtiss Electric propeller has long spinner of the same color as cowl ring and cowl flaps, on Ie Shima, 1945. (Jim Weir via Tom Foote)

Back Cover (bottom right): The front section of the R-2800 engine included a hollow, splined propeller shaft. Some P-47s operated with Hamilton-Standard propellers using oil fed from the engine's oil system to hydraulically actuate prop pitch changes. (Courtesy Ed Baker)

TABLE OF CONTENTS

THE REPUBLIC P-47 THUNDERBOLT

FOREWORD 4
BY COLONEL FRANCIS S. GABRESKI

PREFACE 5
AND THE THANKS GO TO ...

CHAPTER 1: THE BIG IDEA 7
REPUBLIC'S DESIGN OF THE P-47

CHAPTER 2: PRODUCTION 21
P-47S, MODEL BY MODEL

CHAPTER 3: THE BATTLE IS JOINED 45
THUNDERBOLTS IN COMBAT

SPECIAL FULL COLOR SECTION: THE COLOR OF THUNDER 65
P-47 PAINT AND MARKINGS

CHAPTER 4: THUNDERBOLT IN ACTION 69
1944-1945

CHAPTER 5: P-47S AFTER VJ-DAY 87
POSTWAR MILITARY THUNDERBOLTS

CHAPTER 6: CROWD PLEASERS 95
CIVILIAN AND MUSEUM P-47S

APPENDIX A: AMERICAN P-47 UNITS 98

SIGNIFICANT DATES 100
KEY DATES IN THE HISTORY OF THE P-47 THUNDERBOLT

FOREWORD

BY COLONEL FRANCIS S. GABRESKI, USAF (RET.)

Of all the single engine fighters used in combat by the Eighth Air Force, the Thunderbolt was the heaviest but equally the deadliest weapon system integrated into an aeroplane. What made the fighter so successful? Components of a successful war machine. The R-2800 engine was the most powerful aircraft engine then available, turning out 2,000 horsepower. The turbine supercharger maintained the rated power up to 30,000 feet. Its eight machine guns (.50-calibre) gave it firepower unequaled in any fighter weapon system.

The 56th Fighter Group arrived in England with the first combat model of the P-47 in January 1943 and remained with the Thunderbolt throughout the entire war. With constant improvement in the R-2800 engine, the last P-47 model used in Europe was the P-47M. It was the best fighter in the E.T.O. With an increase in power to 2,500 horsepower and considerably lighter, it was a pilot's dream.

The 56th Fighter Group compiled a most enviable combat record, preserved in official 56th Fighter Group documents:

- Destroyed eight enemy aircraft for one loss (8:1)
- Produced 42 aces
- Fifteen aces with 10 or more enemy destroyed
- A total of over 1,000 Luftwaffe pilots fell to the guns of the 56th pilots in the air and on the ground

The 56th Fighter Group was the premiere group in the Eighth Air Force. The P-47 was designed to work with the bombers from 26,000 feet up to 30,000 feet. We fully realized what the advantages were over a much lighter and more maneuverable Luftwaffe fighter. Our strength was hit-and-dive.

What really made the airplane superior was the water injection and paddle blade propeller (introduced during production).

Sincerely,

Gabby Gabreski
May 1999

Col. Francis S. Gabreski smiled from the cockpit of his victory-flag emblazoned P-47 in England. His 28 World War Two victories were unsurpassed in the European Theater of Operations. (Lin Hendrix via SDAM)

Preface

And the Thanks Go To ...

The Republic P-47 Thunderbolt was a single-seat, single-engine fighter, yet in some configurations, its loaded weight could exceed 10 tons. The Thunderbolt towered over its contemporaries, friend and foe. It bucked the trend in U.S. Army Air Forces fighters by using an air-cooled radial engine instead of a slimmer V-12 liquid-cooled powerplant. Not as glamorous as the lithe P-51 Mustang, the P-47 nonetheless earned a reputation for accomplishment — and durability. The barrel-shaped behemoth was bluntly, yet respectfully, called the Jug by its users. In the hands of skilled pilots, the Thunderbolt was a remarkable fighter. Like the otherwise dissimilar P-38 Lightning, the P-47 used a whirring turbosupercharger to gain performance at altitude. Thunderbolts served to the end of World War Two and beyond, playing out their American service lives in Air National Guard squadrons into the early 1950s.

The Army Air Forces and Republic both generated reams of documentation on the P-47, and from these source documents, a glimpse into the Thunderbolt's era can be gleaned. For this book, effort has been made to get under the P-47's skin by digesting its contemporary official reports, many of which have been preserved by the Air Force Historical Research Agency (AFHRA) at Maxwell Air Force Base, Alabama.

This volume includes a variety of assistance from a number of people and organizations, including: Ed Baker, Dana Bell, the Confederate Air Force, Tom Foote, Dan Hagedorn, Ben Howser, Fred LePage, Al Lloyd, David Menard, L. M. Myers, Duane Reed (U.S. Air Force Academy Special Collections), San Diego Aerospace Museum (and Ray Wagner and the museum library staff), and the U.S. Air Force Historical Research Agency. Many of the photos in this volume were printed with care by Koko Partamian at 30-Minute Photo of Palmdale, California. Abbreviations used in some photo captions include AFHRA (Air Force Historical Research Agency), AAF (Army Air Forces), USAF (United States Air Force), USAFA (United States Air Force Academy), and SDAM (San Diego Aerospace Museum).

Author and photographer Warren Bodie deserves notice for his chronicling of the P-47 in text and pictures over many years. Every airplane has its champion.

And very special thanks go to Col. Francis S. Gabreski, the leading living American ace, who shortened the war by 28 German aircraft, while flying a variety of P-47Ds in the 61st Fighter Squadron of the 56th Fighter Group of the Eighth Air Force. Colonel Gabreski is a proud American whose picture should be used in the dictionary next to words like "patriot."

As the drumbeat of the radial engines of World War Two recedes farther into the past, let us not forget the generation of American men and women who built, flew, and maintained Republic P-47 Thunderbolts in their successful bid to help win the incredible global struggle of a world at war.

Frederick A. Johnsen
1999

Sculpted contours of the Thunderbolt are revealed in a photo of a razorback P-47 in England, showing concave dorsal spine aft of the cockpit.
(Fred LePage Collection)

The original purpose for the unusual stores carried by this very low-flying P-47N-15-RE remains unclear, but movie camera installations have not been ruled out. (Peter M. Bowers Collection)

Pictured here is the second of three YP-47Ms (42-27386), altered from a P-47D. The P-47M incorporated the Pratt and Whitney R-2800C engine and CH-5 turbo-supercharger of the fast XP-47J. This "M" series of Thunderbolts were built specifically to combat the fast jet propelled aircraft being used by the German Air Force in the latter months of the European war. (Peter M. Bowers Collection)

THE BIG IDEA

REPUBLIC'S DESIGN OF THE P-47

The Air Force occasionally, whether by intent or not, assigned nomenclature to airplane designs that ultimately bore no resemblance to a later product carrying the same alphanumeric designation. So it was that the XP-47 and XP-47A were "paper airplanes" designed by Republic as lightweight fighters, but never built. They were supposed to embrace the liquid-cooled Allison V-1710 12-cylinder vee-type powerplant then in ascendancy in Air Corps fighter circles. However, Republic engineers led by Alexander Kartveli scrapped the two proposals in favor of their own unique fighter, a radial-engined giant born under the designation XP-47B.

The Republic fighter rationale, reaching back to the days of Alexander P. DeSeversky's influence, typically embraced radial engines to produce pursuits like the then-modern P-35 of 1936 — the first Army single-seat fighter to feature retractable landing gear. The last of 77 P-35s took on a new designation, XP-41, and two notable new features: inward-retracting landing gear instead of the P-35's simple rearward semi-retraction, and, importantly, a turbosupercharger for improved high altitude performance. The XP-41 served as the prototype for a limited-production variant, the P-43 Lancer.[1] Service-test YP-43s were delivered to the Army beginning in September 1940, and ending in April 1941.

The XP-47B's genesis derived from a meeting between Republic Aviation officials and Army Air Forces representatives at Wright Field in the summer of 1940. Then-current fighter designs like the P-43 and another similar Republic experiment, the XP-44, were found wanting in the face of recent European combat experiences. Proposed increases in armament and armor would sorely tax these existing designs, which were powered by radial engines developing at best 1,400 horsepower. Designer Alexander Kartveli and his team of engineers were comfortable with the design rationale of the P-43 and P-44, but they realized a larger engine developing more horsepower was required to propel a combat-worthy airframe. They set about designing a fighter around the huge Pratt and Whitney 2,000 horsepower R-2800 radial engine, with a correspondingly hefty airframe to mate with the big powerplant and carry all the combat equipment necessary. The result was the XP-47B, bearing distinct family traits of the earlier P-44 and P-43 series, but in a bigger, bolder way.

In a compressed schedule that today seems impossible, Kartveli's

The P-43A used an aft ventral location for its turbosupercharger, presaging the layout of the P-47. (Ben Howser Collection)

REPUBLIC
P-47 THUNDERBOLT

7

team conceived, designed, built, and flew the XP-47B prototype in a period of less than a year. First flight was 6 May 1941.[2]

R-2800 Powers the P-47

The use of a radial engine with the XP-47B was a comfortable move for Republic engineers, reflecting their successful evolutions with the P-35 and P-43. The Thunderbolt prototype's performance validated their faith in radials.

The Pratt and Whitney 18-cylinder, twin-row radial R-2800 air-cooled engine propelled the Thunderbolt, following the smaller P-43's use of another Pratt and Whitney product, the R-1830 engine. Total piston displacement of the R-2800 was 2,804 cubic inches. Some R-2800 models had provision for a gun synchronizer to keep bullets from striking the propeller, but for the P-47, all eight wing guns were aligned outboard of the propeller arc. To derive power from the rapidly-firing 18 cylinders, the R-2800 employed a crankshaft machined from three steel forgings, bolted together.[3]

The R-2800 was rugged, and not dependent on a liquid coolant system. In fact, a 1943 AAF tactical evaluation of the P-47C, in discussing armor protection for the Thunderbolt pilot, said: "The engine also affords good protection."[4] Thunderbolts limped back to base with severe engine damage that would have seized up a liquid-cooled powerplant.

When some Ninth Air Force Thunderbolt R-2800-10 engines in storage were found to have internal rust, the AAF Materiel Command advised users: "Those engines with moderate rust on cylinder walls, link and master rods, and on the spiders that retain the knuckle pins, can be operated with little likelihood of failure. Results of tests run effectively support the decision made to leave the R-2800-10 with possible rusting inside in service until normal overhaul time."[5] Abilities like this earned the R-2800 a justified measure of loyalty and trust among pilots and crew chiefs.

The P-47C engine was said by the

The P-43's conventional cockpit location was accommodated by the aft ventral location of the airplane's turbosupercharger. Upended example (serial 40-2920) was photographed at Oregon's Portland Air Base on 19 January 1942. (Ben Howser Collection)

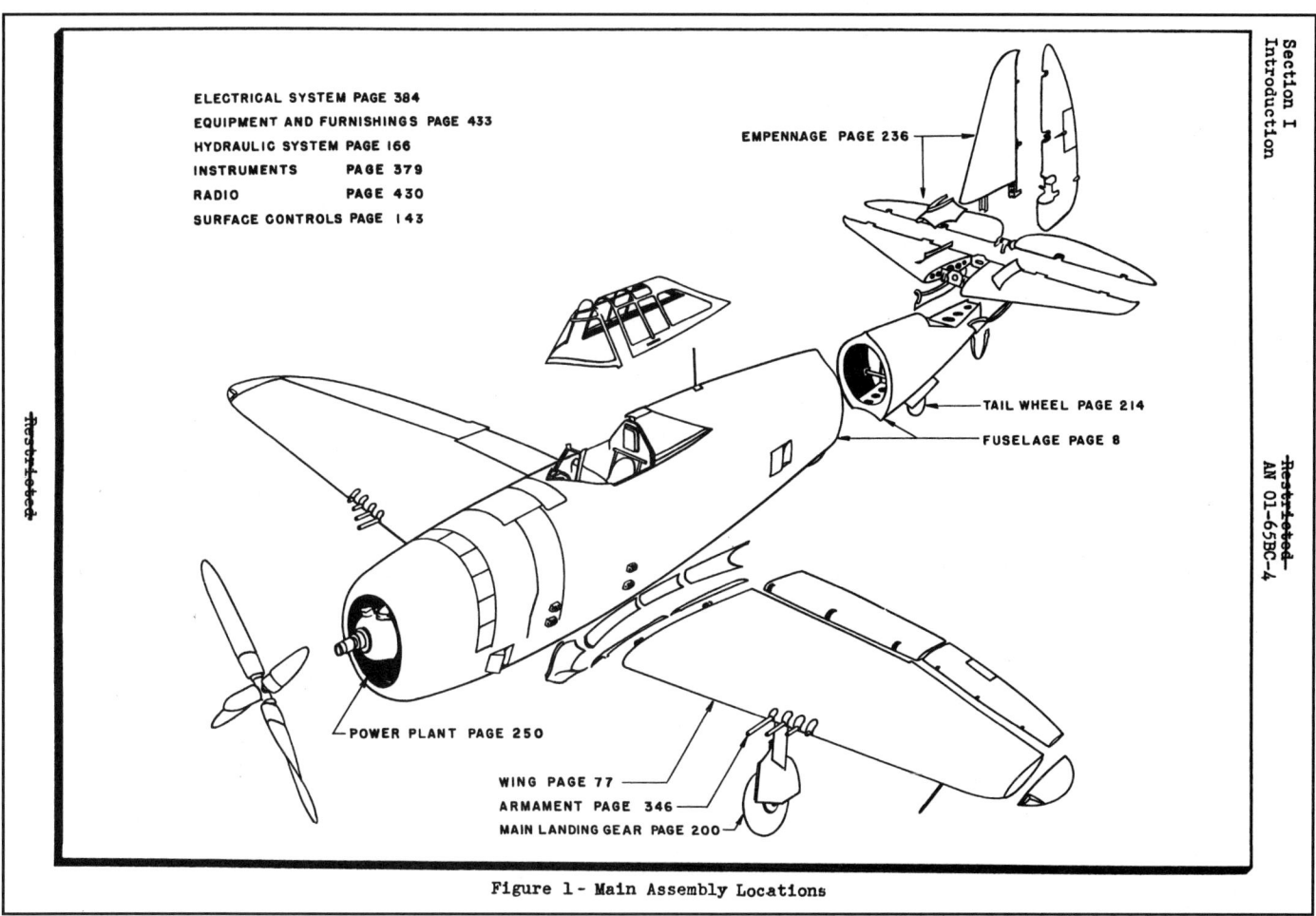

Exploded view from a P-47 "Dash-4" illustrated parts catalog shows main components of a typical razorback Thunderbolt. Entire trailing edge of wing was consumed by flaps and ailerons. (AAF)

AAF to be "exceptionally easy to start provided the correct instructions are followed. The starter is so quiet and smooth that it is difficult to tell it is energizing. The engine warms up rapidly and requires about 45 seconds to start for a 'Scramble' take-off."[6]

The starter may have been smooth, but reports of excessive vibration in some P-47s led Republic to install new soft core dynafocal engine mounts beginning with P-47D-23-RA serial number 42-25869 and P-47D-25RE serial 42-26724. The six soft core mounts could be retrofitted to other P-47s.[7]

The P-43 addressed weight-and-balance issues regarding its turbosupercharger by placing the turbo in the aft fuselage, connected to the engine by long ducting. This allowed for a more conventional cockpit placement than had been achieved with the Curtiss turbosupercharged P-37, with the engine and turbo up front, well ahead of a displaced aft cockpit that was considered operationally unsuitable. The P-47 Thunderbolt continued the use of an aft location for the turbo.[8]

Chasing Mach One

A number of Thunderbolt pilots and test pilots from several venues

P-35, P-43, AND P-47 STATISTICAL COMPARISON				
MODEL	SPAN	LENGTH	GROSS WEIGHT	TOP SPEED
P-35	36 ft.	25 ft., 2 in.	5599 lbs.	280 mph
P-43A	36 ft.	28 ft., 6 in.	7435 lbs.	356 mph
P-47B	40 ft., 9 in.	35 ft.	13,360 lbs.	429 mph

Engineless Thunderbolt training aid showed exhaust collector ring for R-2800 engine, and large carburetor air duct that piped air forward, along the side of the cockpit, from the turbosupercharger in the aft fuselage to the engine. (AAF)

Ambient air was ducted to the aft-located turbosupercharger where it was compressed and fed forward in two pipes to the P-47's engine carburetor, as depicted in a Thunderbolt illustrated parts book. (AAF)

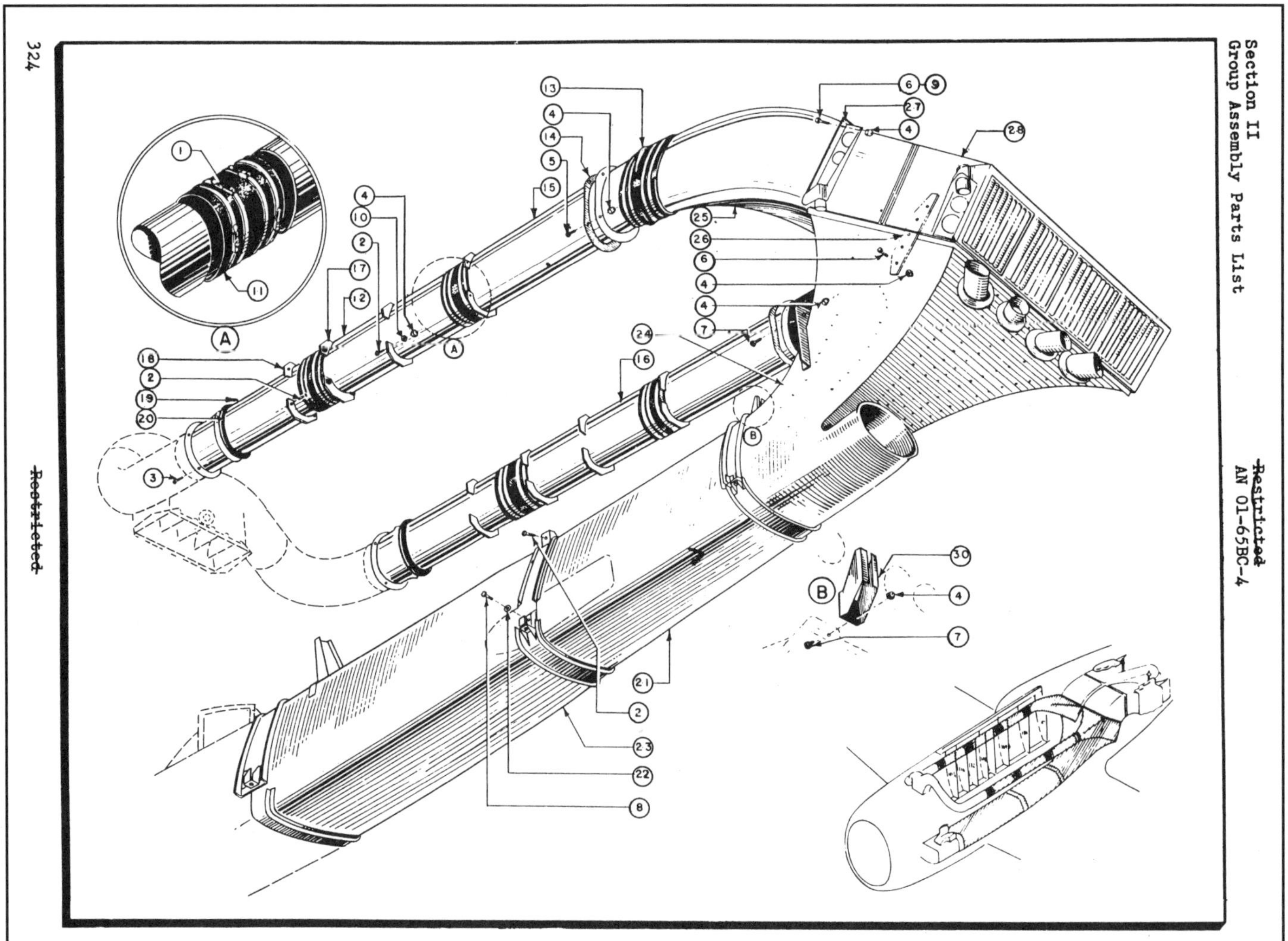

Figure 163 - Supercharger System Installation

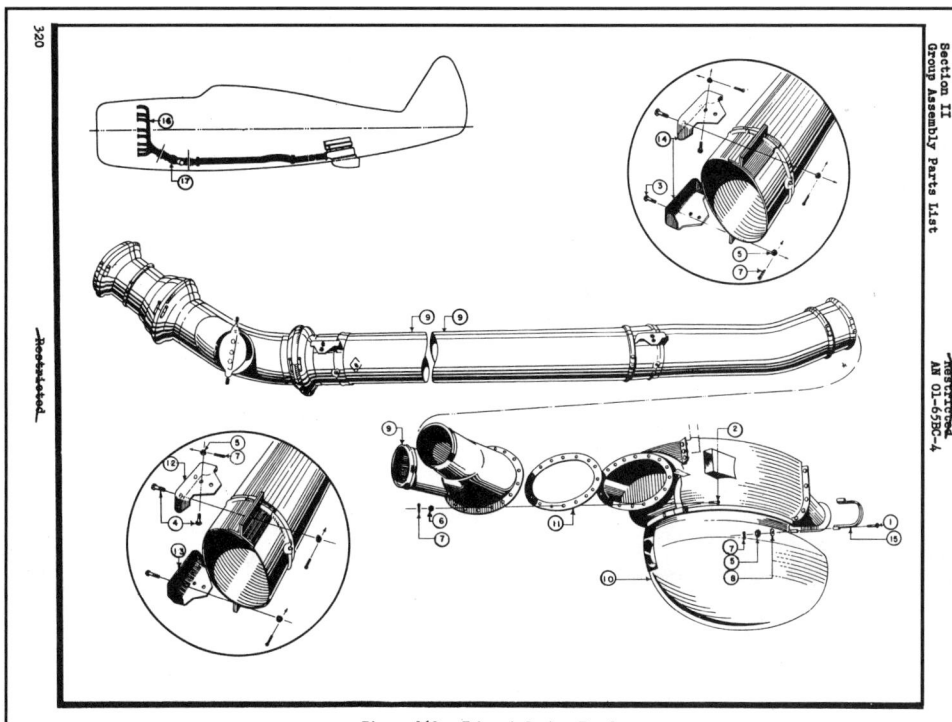

The P-47 collector ring sent exhaust gas aft in pipes inside the fuselage, where its energy spun the turbine that operated the turbosupercharger before exiting. (AAF)

P-47 exhaust pipes were shrouded along the belly of the fuselage before joining just ahead of the turbosupercharger, according to a drawing from a Thunderbolt illustrated parts book. (AAF)

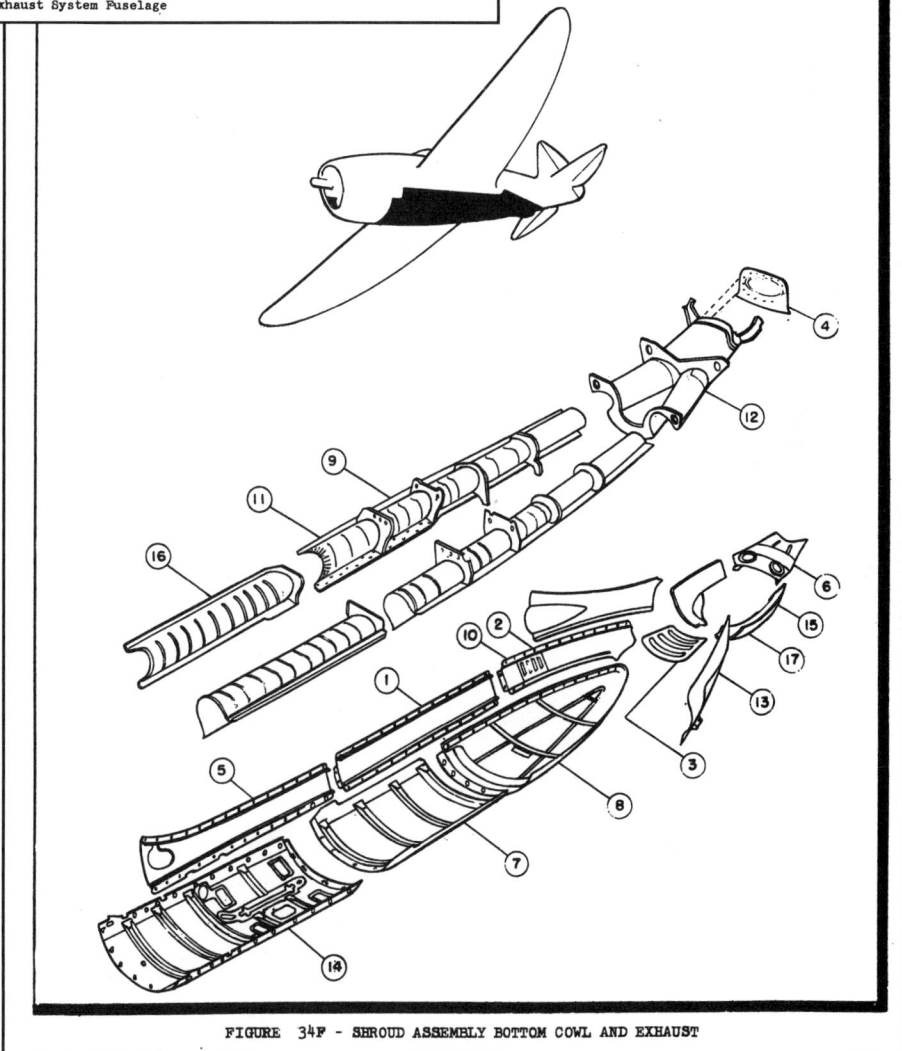

concur: The piston-engine fighters of World War Two could *not* fly faster than sound. And yet a story persisted for many years that the P-47 could fall out of the sky in a screaming dive fast enough to exceed the speed of sound.

One player in this story must surely be a Republic Aviation news release dated 1 December 1942 which proclaimed: "New aerodynamic and speed frontiers were established November 15 at an East Coast Air Base when two Army lieutenants, in Republic P-47 Thunderbolts, dived these powerful fighter planes at 725 miles an hour, and probably became the first human beings to hurtle through space at a speed greater than that of sound." One of the pilots was quoted as saying he used the elevator trim to effect a pullout when the stick became rigid. The company news release eloquently stated: "While both of their speeds are listed officially at 725, it is quite likely that … (one of the pilots) … exceeded that figure and touched that mystical realm where the airflow spatters and sound waves begin to act on control surfaces — with unpredictable results."[9]

In fairness, the whole transonic region was new territory for aviators. And while the P-47 was definitely capable of diving into the region where airflow was disturbed by transonic phenomena, this was new and somewhat imprecise science in 1942. If Republic may have jumped the gun on claiming that a P-47 flew faster than sound, we now have the benefit of hindsight that they could not possess at the time. The plucky fliers who made those hurtling dives helped expand the frontiers of high-speed flight.

The ultimate Thunderbolt model, the P-47N, came with advice to pilots on treating the phenomenon of shock wave compressibility, when air flowing at high speeds over the top of the wing altered airflow characteristics across the tail as the Thunderbolt nudged into the transonic — not supersonic — speed regime. Two symptoms of the onset of compressibility in a dive were a "nose heavy" tuck under tendency and increasing stiffness in the elevators. The P-47N pilot training manual advised: "To avoid it, pull the nose up slowly and gradually reduce airspeed." Contrary to some of the tricks tried by the 1942 pilots in the Republic news release, the P-47N manual said: "If you actually get into compressibility, use the following procedure to recover:

1. Apply strong back pressure on the stick.
2. Keep the ailerons neutral.
3. Keep the ball centered (on the turn-and-bank indicator).
4. Increase power, never decrease.
5. Do not use elevator trim. Keep the ailerons in neutral. Moving the stick to either side will not aid your recovery and will probably get you into trouble."[10]

P-47N pilots were cautioned to ensure rudder trim was neutral if they were in compressibility conditions to avoid dangerous strains on the tail. With a neutral rudder trim

The R-2800 engine defined the Thunderbolt. Twin rows of cylinders produced 2,000 horsepower in the Pratt and Whitney powerplant. Front of engine is at right in the photo. (AAF)

The front section of the R-2800 engine included a hollow, splined propeller shaft. Some P-47s operated with Hamilton-Standard propellers using oil fed from the engine's oil system to hydraulically actuate prop pitch changes. (Courtesy Ed Baker)

Cutaway view of the R-2800 engine showed the piston rods, and push rod, rocker, and valve set-up. (Courtesy Ed Baker)

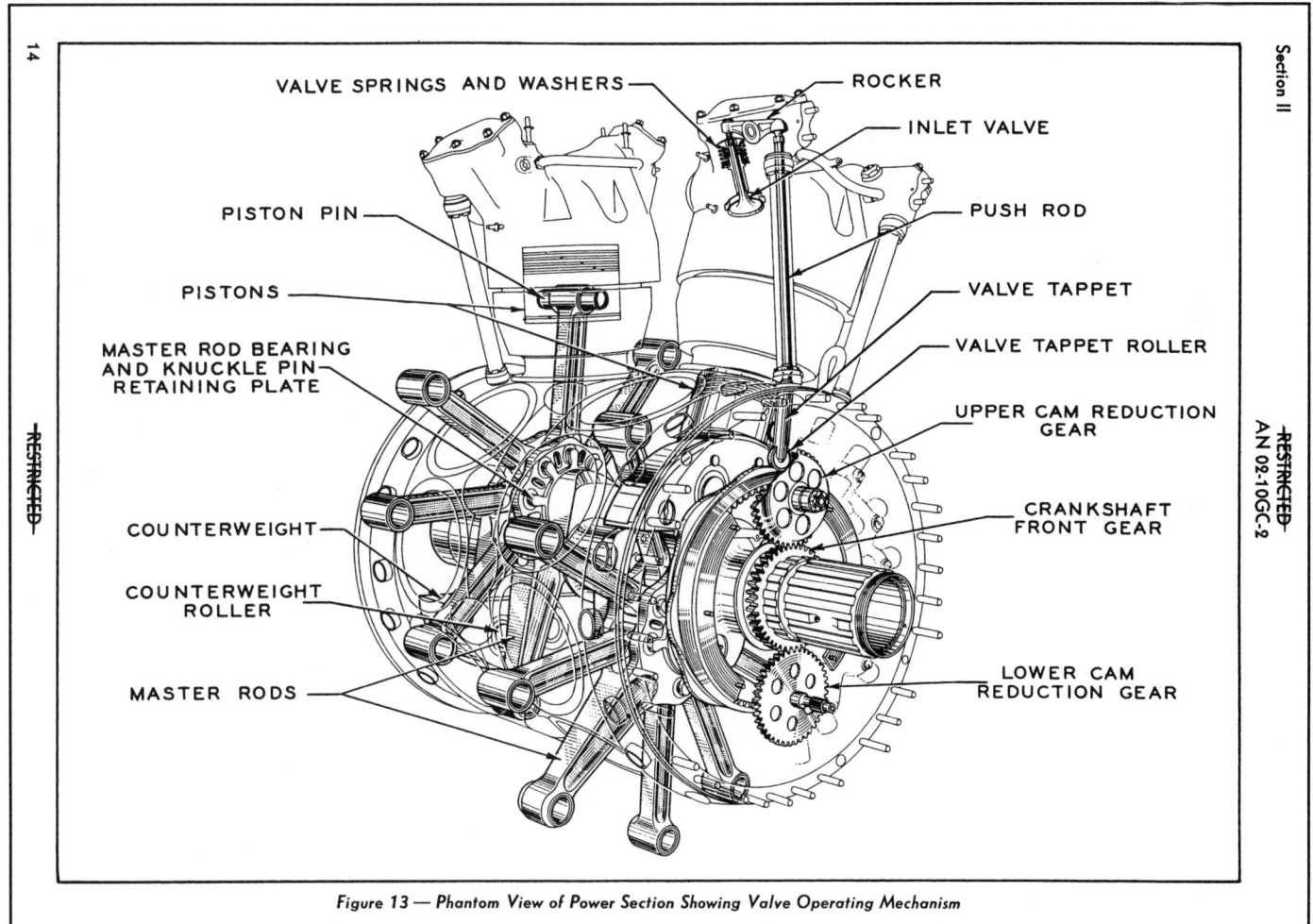

Figure 5 — Three-quarter Cutaway View of Front Section (.450:1 Reduction Gearing)

Figure 13 — Phantom View of Power Section Showing Valve Operating Mechanism

Gripping the leading edge of the wing for support against the punishing prop wash, a mechanic worked on a P-47 during a ground engine run. Large left side carburetor air duct elbow is visible where cowling has been removed. (AAF)

setting, the rudder had a tendency to streamline itself. "Don't cut the throttle to slow up," the manual instructed. "It will only steepen your dive by making the nose drop. Increase power to raise the nose." The pilot who found himself in a compressibility dive was told to pull back hard on the control stick. "Don't jerk it. Just keep a steady pressure, as strong as you can make it against the locking effect of compressibility," the manual explained. As an aircraft hurtles toward earth, it encounters denser air which actually decreases the grip of compressibility by raising the speed at which it can begin. In lower, denser air, the combination of power-on and steady stick back pressure could finally pull the errant Thunderbolt out of its dive.

"The elevator trim tab is not effective when the airplane is in compressibility," the manual reported. "If you use it, the only result will be an extremely violent pull-out when you recover." P-47N pilots were cautioned: "Never start a dive pulling more than cruising horsepower. This gives you a margin of additional power without danger of exceeding the red line. The added air ram of a high speed dive increases your manifold pressure and makes it mighty easy to exceed the limits." Some aircraft incorporated dive flaps on the undersurfaces of the wing to alter airflow characteristics as a way of breaking the grip of compressibility; because of its long-range internal wing fuel tanks, the P-47N could not be fitted with compressibility recovery flaps, the manual noted.[11]

Even though the mighty Thunderbolt could not break the sound barrier, its fearsome compressibility dives warranted scientific investigation. The loss of the XP-47B in a high speed dive in August 1942 only added to the questions about high speed phenomena. In September and October 1942, the 20-foot wind tunnel at Wright Field studied a full-size P-47B tail section. According to an AAF summary: "The object

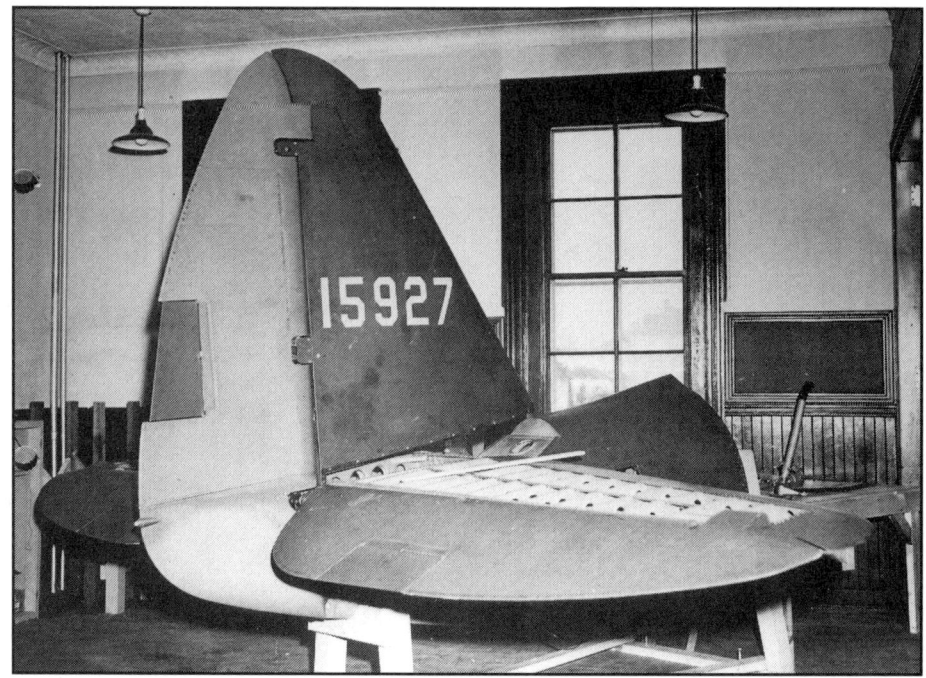

The tail section from P-47B 41-5927, used as a training aid, included fabric covering on the control surfaces; later Thunderbolt control surfaces were metal clad. (AFHRA)

of this test was to investigate the effect of Mach Number on the pressure distribution and, also, to investigate the effect of model attitude and surface deflection on the pressure distribution."[12]

The tail section tested consisted of the complete empennage and a little over nine-and-a-half feet of the aft fuselage of a P-47B. Control surfaces of the B-model were fabric covered. The vertical fin, rudder, and the lefthand horizontal stabilizer and elevator were fitted with a total of 295 flush-mounted pressure orifices connected to instrumentation. The tail assembly was mounted on a six-component balance capable of measuring lift, drag, pitch, yaw, roll, and side force acting on the model. Data gleaned from the test was to be used "in a general study of the adequacy of present design load requirements for tail surfaces at high Mach Numbers."[13]

After the P-47Bs, production Thunderbolts starting with the P-47C had metal-clad control surfaces.

Check Six

The classic fighter pilot's warning, "Check Six," means to look to the rear, to the six o'clock position, for a possible threat. During 1943, a P-47 participated in tests of a 20-pound AN/APS-13 radar set that did just that. Visible as three quarter-inch metal rods piercing the vertical fin, and extending out for about five and a quarter inches on either side, the radar provided warning of the approach of aircraft behind the equipped Thunderbolts. Within a cone of space behind the P-47, any aircraft approaching closer than 800 yards was announced. The cone radiated through about 60 degrees horizontally and 90 degrees vertically behind the Thunderbolt. The cone of coverage was slightly skewed upward, to enhance detection of diving aircraft. Given limitations on radar technology, the system was useless at altitudes below 800 yards, an AAF test summary explained, "since it is practically impossible to prevent spurious radiation from returning from the earth's surface."[14]

Upon detection of an aircraft in the rear cone of space, a brilliant red jeweled light in a shield beside the P-47's gunsight illuminated, letting the pilot know instantly of the presence of an aircraft which might pose a threat. The tail-warning radar was tested initially mounted in a twin-engine Beech AT-11, followed by installation in a P-47.[15]

Following encouraging tests with one P-47, six follow-on AN/APS-13 tail warning radars were installed at Orlando, Florida, in Thunderbolts of Squadron F of the 904th AAF Base Unit stationed at Kissimmee Army Air Base, Florida. An AAF paper explained: "The position and arrangement of the antenna on the stabilizer determines the tilt of the cone with respect to the airplane." The six sets installed in Orlando

Mounting a razorback P-47C in England in 1943 was 2nd Lt. James Richard Carter of the 56th Fighter Group. Lever handgrip aided ascent by an equipment-laden flier. (AAF via Fred LePage Collection)

also featured an alarm bell that sounded when the warning light was illuminated.[16]

A staple of Cold War jet fighters, tail warning radar proved its utility on a handful of P-47s during World War Two.

What a Performance

Thunderbolt chronicler Warren Bodie has noted that an experimental laminar-flow wing which was fitted to the XP-47F in the hopes of increasing performance actually diminished the numbers below the figures for a standard P-47B or C-model. Author Bodie suggests the burgeoning Republic Aviation company was fully occupied with the gargantuan tasks of mass-producing standard Thunderbolts, and the nuances of laminar flow design, which demanded strict adherence to a critical airfoil profile, and a skin surface free of blemishes, were difficult to control in the hectic production schedules maintained during World War Two. That the Thunderbolt was a 400-mile-per-hour single-engine fighter *without* the vaunted laminar flow wing is a testimonial to the Republic design team of Alexander Kartveli and D. Weed.[17]

[1] Peter M. Bowers, *Forgotten Fighters and Experimental Aircraft — Vol. 2, U.S. Army, 1918-1941*, Arco, New York, New York, 1971. [2] *P-47 Thunderbolt – The Jug*, The P-47 Thunderbolt Pilots Association, New York, New York, (Dave Turner and Associates, Paducah, Kentucky; Taylor Publishing Company, Dallas Texas) 1981. [3] "Service Instructions for Aircraft Engines Models R-2800-14W, -22, -22W, -34, -34W, -57, -73, -77, -81, -83 and -85," AN 02-10GC-2, 5 August 1945, Revised 15 November 1946. [4] "Tactical Employment Trials on the Republic Airplane P-47C," Report of the Army Air Forces Board, AAFSAT, Orlando, Florida, 16 February 1943. [5] Memorandum, "P-47 Maintenance and Modification Notes," Headquarters, IX Tactical Air Command, to Commanding Officers, All P-47 Groups, *et al*, 9 August 1944. [6] "Tactical Employment Trials on the Republic Airplane P-47C," Report of the Army Air Forces Board, AAFSAT, Orlando, Florida, 16 February 1943. [7] Memorandum, "P-47 Maintenance and Modification Notes," Headquarters, IX Tactical Air Command, to Commanding Officers, All P-47 Groups, *et al*, 9 August 1944. [8] Benjamin S. Kelsey, *The Dragon's Teeth? The Creation of United States Air Power for World War II*, Smithsonian Institution Press, Washington, D.C., 1982. [9] Untitled story about high-speed P-47 dives, by Republic Aviation Public Relations, dated 1 December 1942 (filed at U.S. Air Force Historical Research Agency, Maxwell AFB, Alabama). [10] *Pilot Training Manual for the Thunderbolt P-47N*, AAF, circa 1945. [11] *Ibid*. [12] Army Air Forces Technical Report, 20-Foot Wind Tunnel Test No. 14: "20-Foot Wind Tunnel Pressure Distribution Measurements on the Full Scale Tail Surfaces of the Republic P-47B Airplane," War Department, Army Air Forces, Materiel Center, Wright Field, Dayton, Ohio, 13 May 1943. [13] *Ibid*. [14] Report of the Army Air Forces Board, "Final Report on Test of Tail Warning Device for Fighter Aircraft," Project No. (M-3) 15, 2 October 1943. [15] *Ibid*. [16] Memo, Army Air Forces Board Project No. 3584B452.04, "Test of the Tactical Suitability of an AN/APS-13 Tail-Warning Radar Installed in Fighter Aircraft," 30 December 1944. [17] Warren M. Bodie, *Thunderbolt*, Wings Special Edition No. 1, Sentry Books, Granada Hills, California.

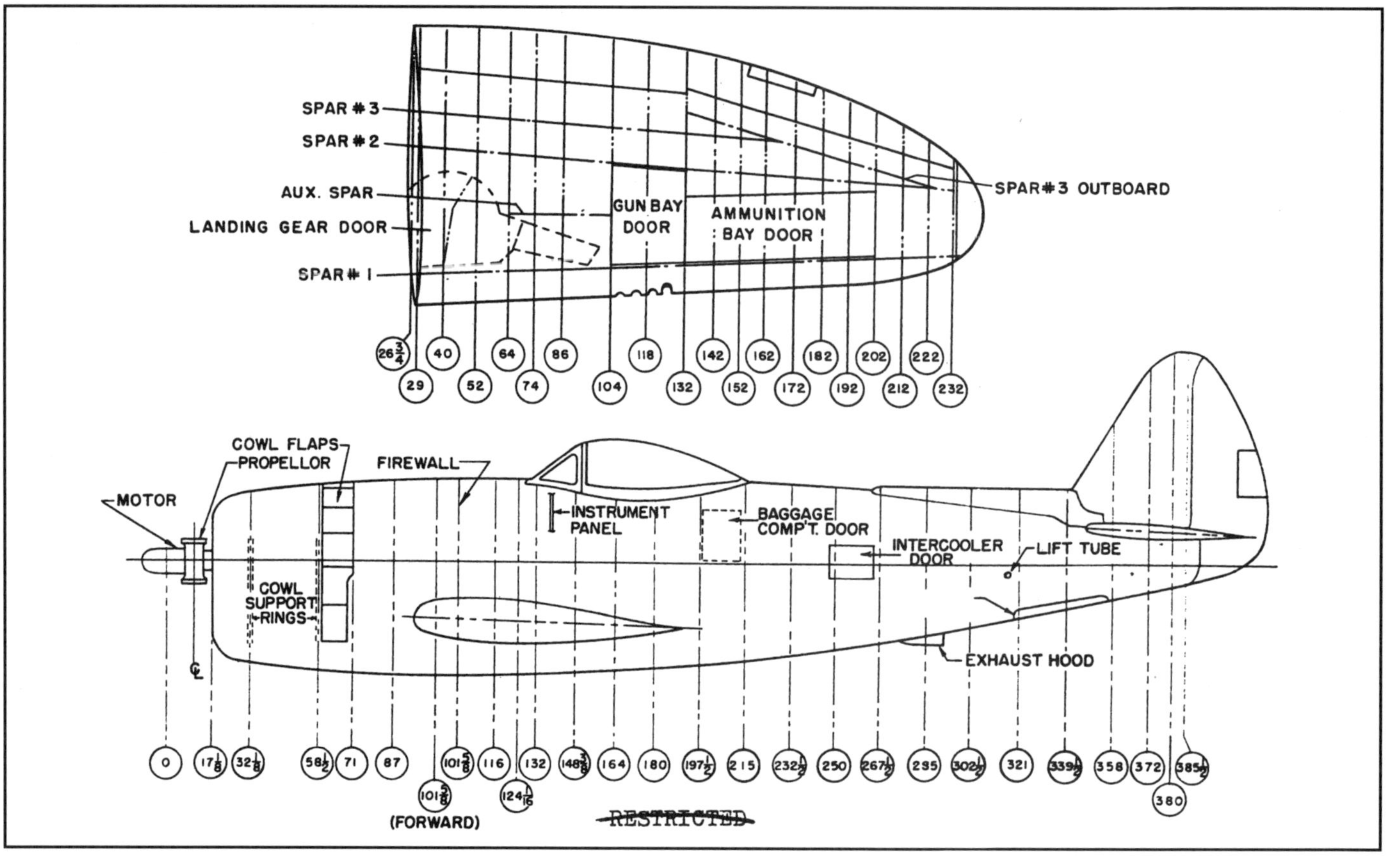

Station diagram for bubble-top P-47D shows access doors, placement of instrument panel, and turbosupercharger exhaust hood. (AAF)

SECTION II—GROUP ASSEMBLY PARTS LISTS

AN 01-65BC-4A

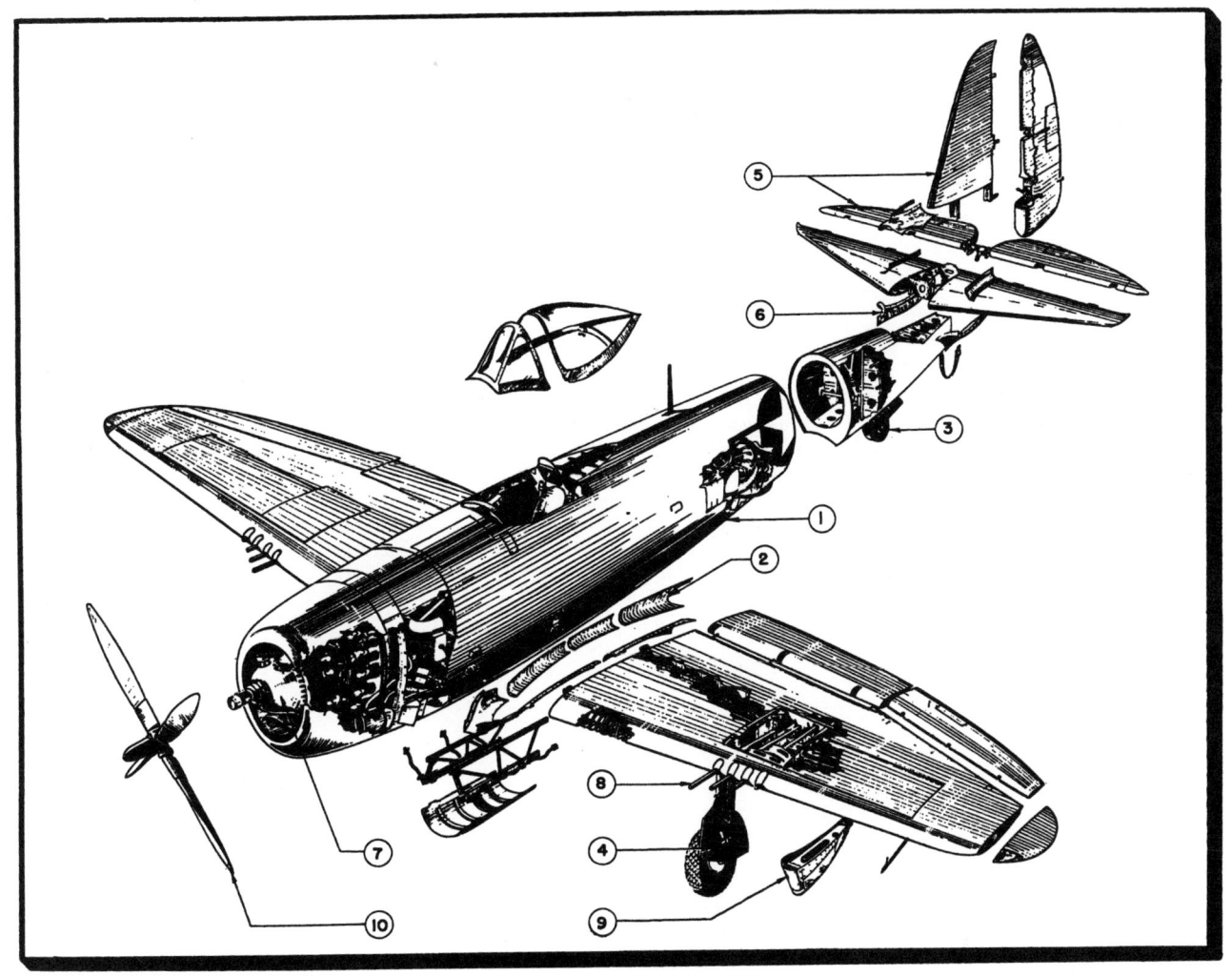

Figure 1 - General Assembly

FIG. NO.	INDEX NO.	STOCKED	GROUP / MAJOR ASSEMBLY / PART NUMBER	GENERAL ASSEMBLY / MAJOR INSTALLATION						UNITS PER ASSY	PROPERTY CLASSIFICATION		
				1	2	3	4	5	6	NOMENCLATURE		U.S. NAVY	U.S. ARMY	BRITISH
			*93X10200	General Assembly									
1	1		93F12000	Fuselage Assembly - Complete							1	0123	126JR
1	2		89X27300-57	Fillets Installation - Wing							1	0123	126JR
1	3		93M42000	Wheel Installation - Tail							1	0123	126JR
1	4		89L43000L	Fairing Installation - Landing Gear (Left)							1	0123	126JR
1	4		89L43000R	Fairing Installation - Landing Gear (Right)							1	0123	126JR
1	5		89E51000	Empennage Installation							1	0123	126JR
1	6		89X56000	Fillets Installation - Empennage							1	0123	126JR
1	7		93X61005	Power Plant Installation							1	0123	126JR
1	8		93X71000	Armament Installation							1	0123	126JR
1	9		93X78130L	Adapter Installation - Wing Tank (Left)							1	0123	126JR
1	9		93X78130R	Adapter Installation - Wing Tank (Right)							1	0123	126JR
1	10		C542SA34	Propeller (Curtiss) (GFE)							1	4006	125A

Exploded view of bubble-top P-47D from an illustrated parts book depicts underwing shackle (part 9).(AAF)

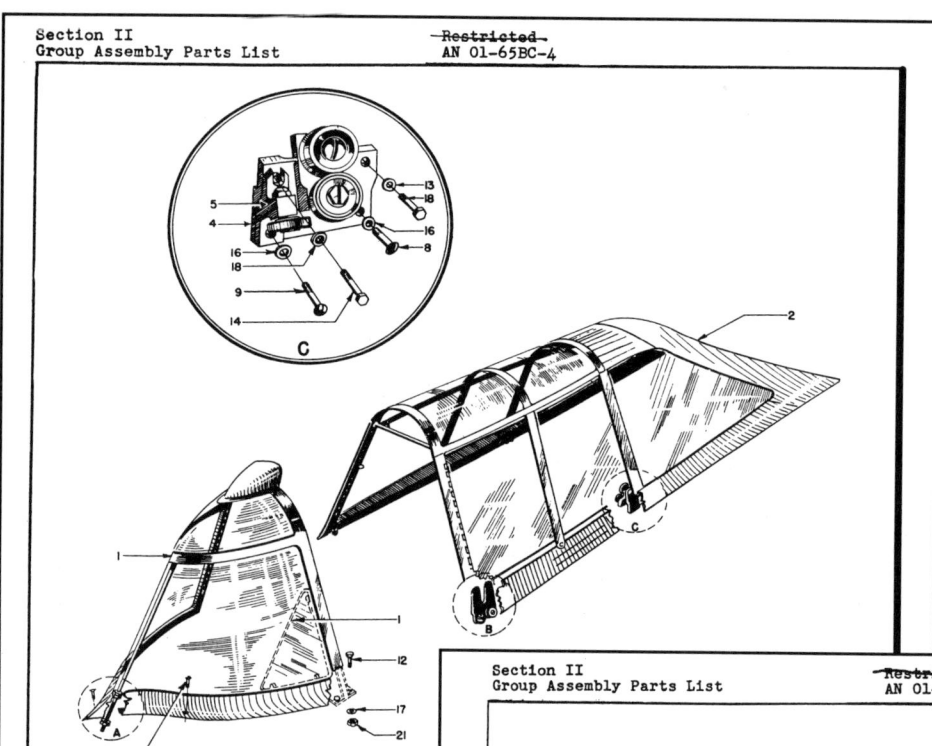

Canopy and windscreen of razorback Thunderbolts showed similarities to earlier P-43 glazing. V-shaped windscreen was found to shed raindrops well. (AAF)

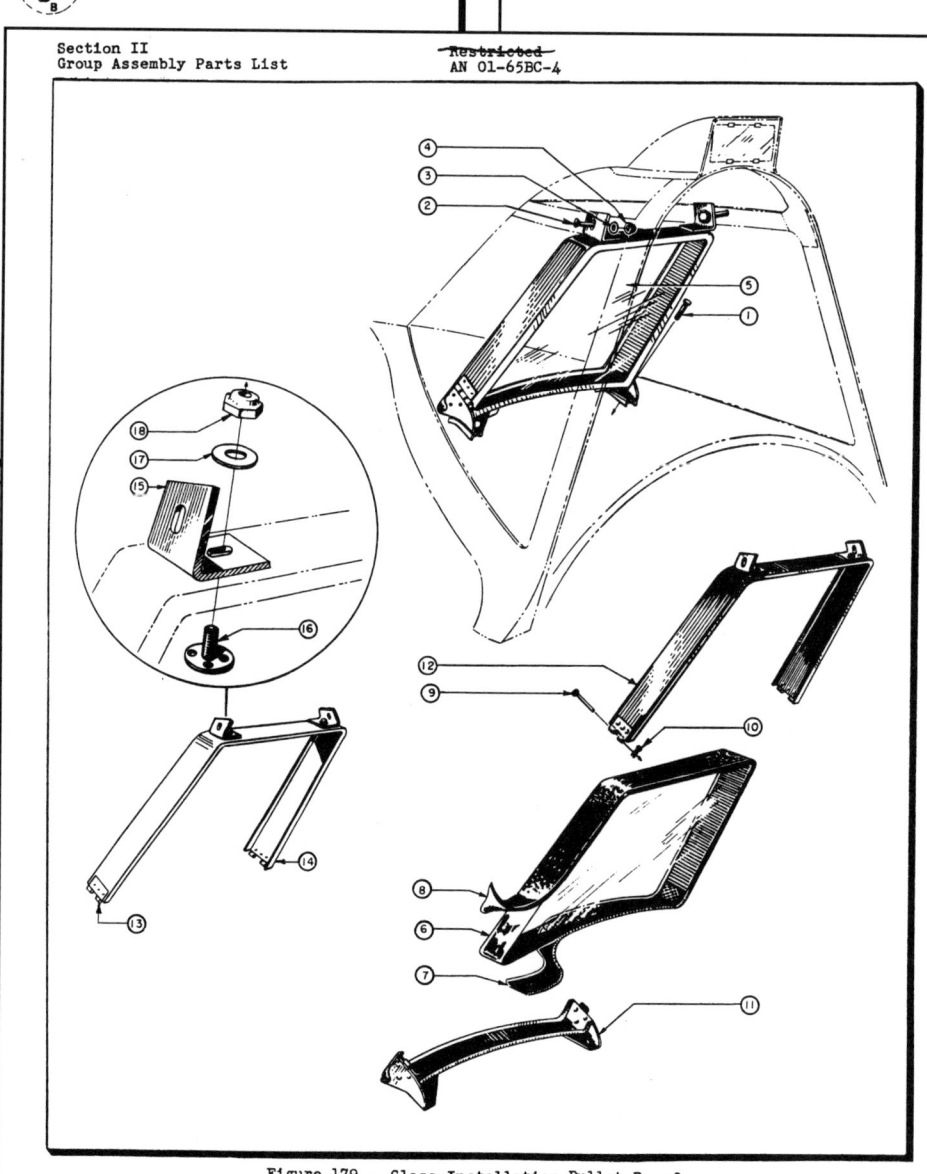

Figure 179 – Glass Installation Bullet Proof

Razorback P-47Cs and D-models with knife-edge v-shaped windscreen were fitted with internal front armor glass (part number 5), mounted in a padded and felt-lined metal frame. (AAF)

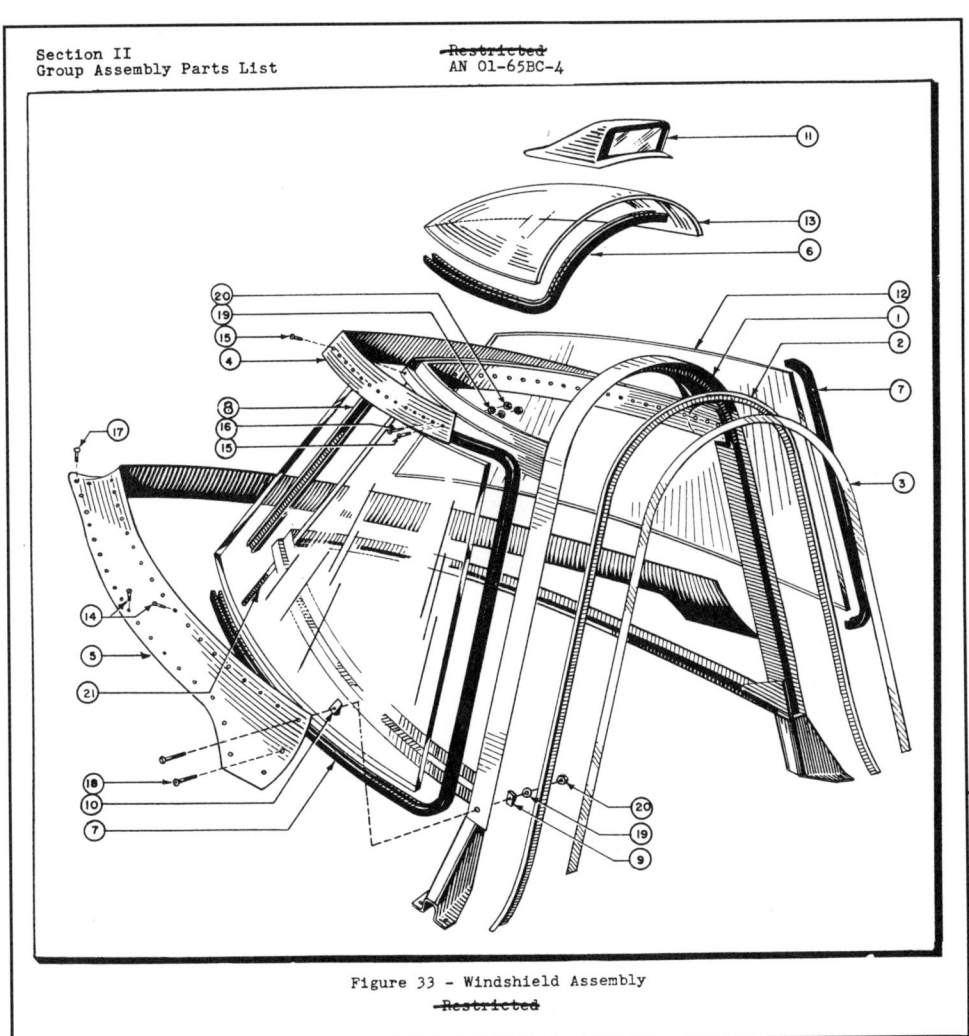

Many parts made up the knife-edge windscreen assembly of razorback Thunderbolts. Rearview mirror (part number 11) was housed in a streamlined fairing. (AAF)

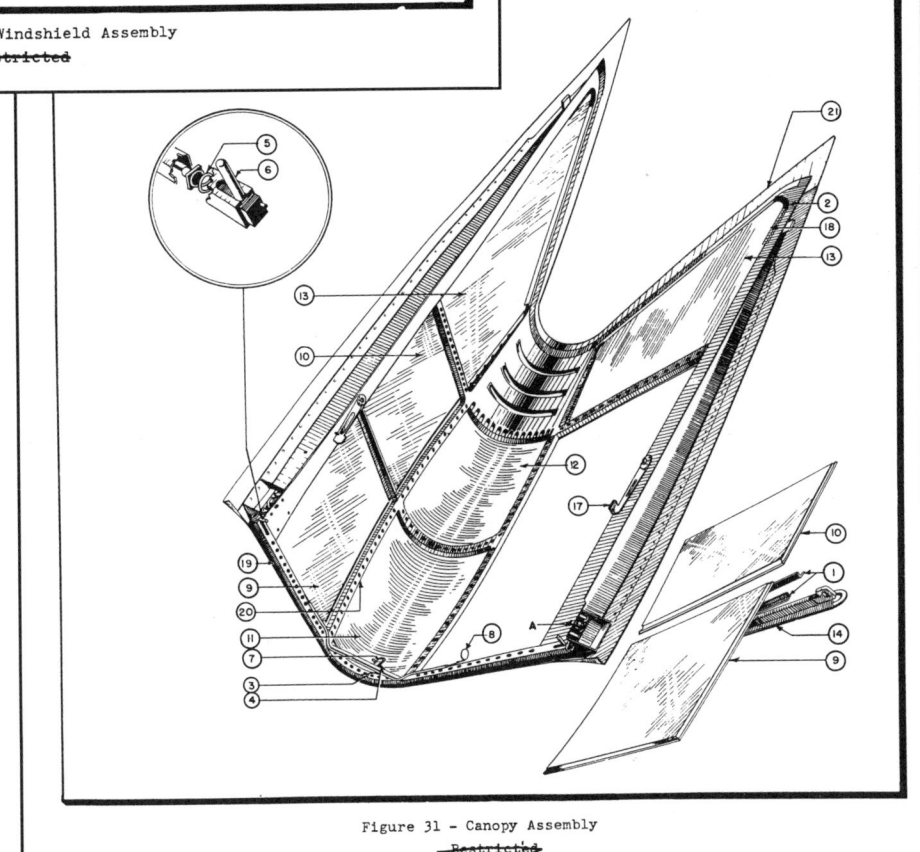

Inside view from parts book shows razorback P-47 canopy construction details. (AAF)

REPUBLIC P-47 THUNDERBOLT

19

Incredible view of distorted P-47D horizontal stabilizer shows collateral battle damage pock marks on vertical fin as well. (AAF)

Mechanics swarmed P-47C number 41-6622 on a fire extinguisher-foamed runway after its 18 August 1943 engine blaze. (AFHRA)

P-47C number 41-6622 suffered a serious engine fire that burned through the cowling and fuselage on 18 August 1943 in England. (AAF/Fred LePage)

PRODUCTION 2

P-47s, Model by Model

With the lightweight XP-47 and XP-47A interceptor proposals stillborn, the first actual aircraft to carry the nomenclature was the XP-47B (serial number 40-3051). Test pilot Lowery L. Brabham first took the XP-47B aloft on 6 May 1941. It was a behemoth that mocked any notion of light weight at more than six tons on the scales. Where the Royal Air Force — a likely potential customer — was favorably disposed to fighters mounting four machine guns in each wing, the XP-47B upped the ante from typical light British .303-caliber weapons to beefy American M-2 .50-caliber machine guns. This would give the Thunderbolt a fearsome and withering ground-attack presence as well as putting forth a curtain of lethal fire in air-to-air engagements. The XP-47B's big radial XR-2800-21 engine issued 2,000 horsepower, and gave the prototype Thunderbolt a promising top speed of 412 miles an hour.[1]

The production P-47Bs that followed used a sliding cockpit canopy in place of the XP-47B's hinging side panel. In later years, fighter designers would decry the "pound-a-day diet", implying the rate at which weight seemed to bloom on fighter designs as they metamorphosed from testbed prototype to operational production variants. The production P-47B had a gross weight of 13,356 pounds, but production versions of the R-2800-21 engine were even more capable than the powerplant of the prototype, and production B-models could hit an impressive 429 miles an hour.

The P-47C could carry a 200-gallon centerline drop tank, or alternately, a 500-pound bomb. The C-model also was stretched by 13 inches to promote better maneuverability. Ultimately, extending the motor mounts about eight inches altered the center of gravity to the benefit of subsequent Thunderbolts. The production run of C-models totaled 602 aircraft, many of which were destined for European combat duty.

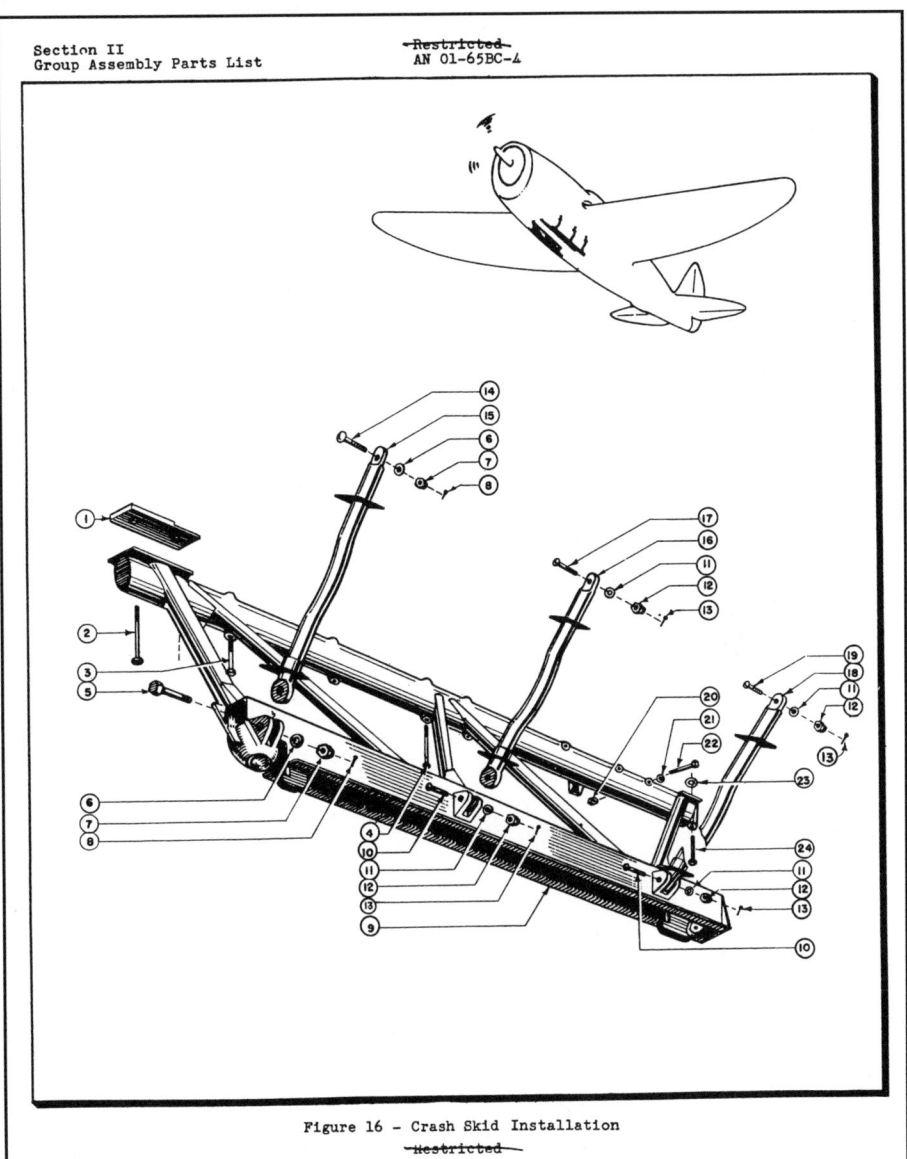

Internal crash skid installation enhanced structural integrity of Thunderbolt in wheels-up landings. (AAF)

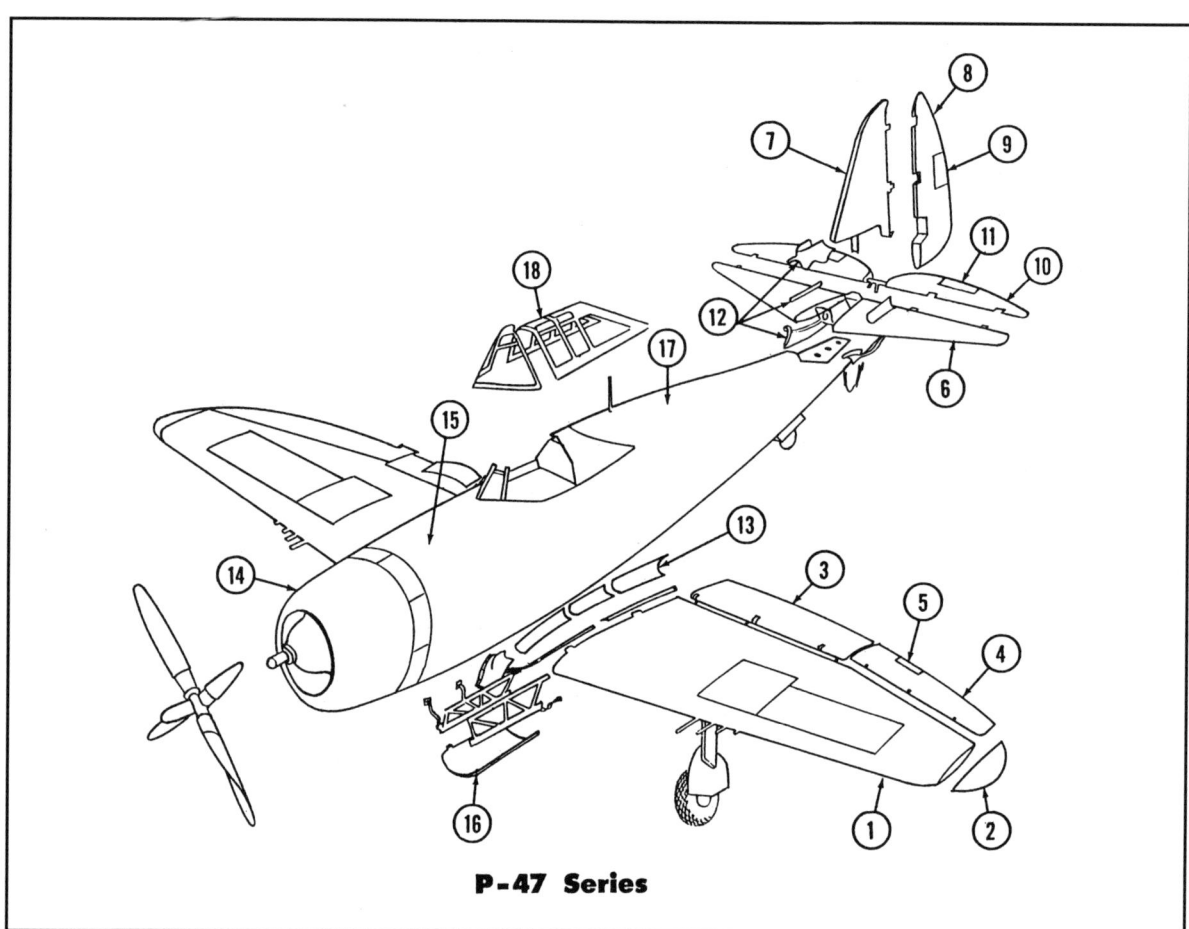

One of several exploded views of P-47s drawn for wartime technical manuals shows fairing (part 16) and crash skids. (Bill Miranda Collection)

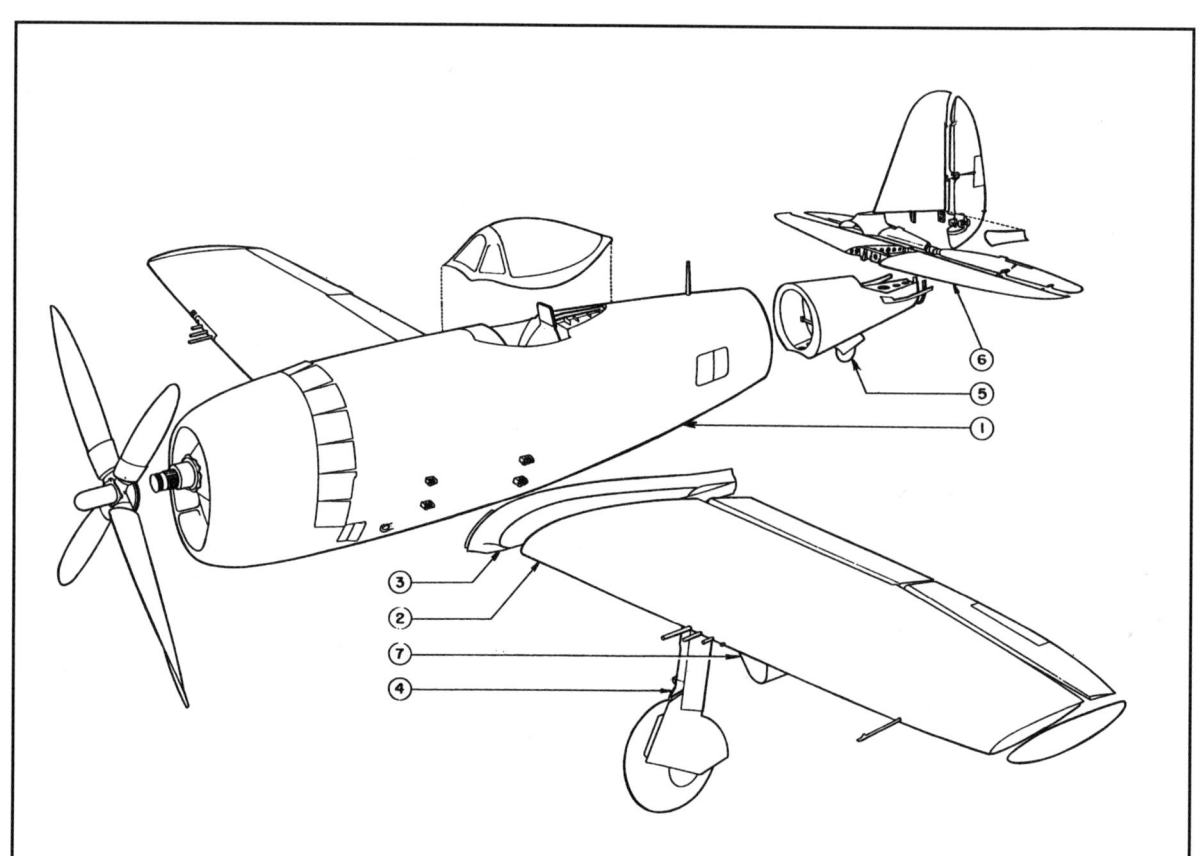

Early P-47N depiction shows clipped wingtips, but no dorsal fin, which was applied to this model Thunderbolt. (AAF)

As described in an AAF evaluation report: "The main differences in the P-47C as compared with the P-47B are: moving the engine eight inches forward, quick detachable engine mount, metal covered control surfaces, and strengthened tail structure. These changes increase the weight of the P-47C by approximately 900 pounds."[2]

The AAF report further detailed the C-model Thunderbolt: "The Republic P-47C is a high altitude (20,000 to 30,000 feet) single seater, single engine, low wing fighter armed with four free-firing .50-calibre machine guns in each wing. The power plant is a Pratt and Whitney R-2800-21 twin row 18 cylinder, supercharged, air cooled engine of 2,000 h.p. It is provided with gear driven first stage and turbine driven second stage superchargers; the turbine driven supercharger is a separate unit with its R.P.M. controlled by optional linkage with the throttle or by a separate lever. The power plant drives a four bladed Curtiss electrically controlled constant speed propeller."[3]

All three landing gear, the brakes, wing flaps, and cowl flaps were hydraulically actuated. For takeoff in the P-47C, the AAF evaluation explained, "the tail wheel should be locked by means of a lever, located on the bottom front right side of the cockpit. The tail wheel automatically locks when the landing gear is lowered; therefore, it must be released at the end of the landing run in order to taxi." (The ability of the tailwheel to swivel was needed for taxiing turns, but for takeoff and landing, the wheel was kept from swiveling to maintain the P-47 on a straight heading down the runway.)

If the P-47C pilot could not get the landing gear to lower hydraulically, he could let the gear fall out of the wheel wells aided by gravity. Then, to ensure the main gear had locked in place, the pilot could skid the aircraft's flight path in both directions to let wind blast against the mainwheels and gear

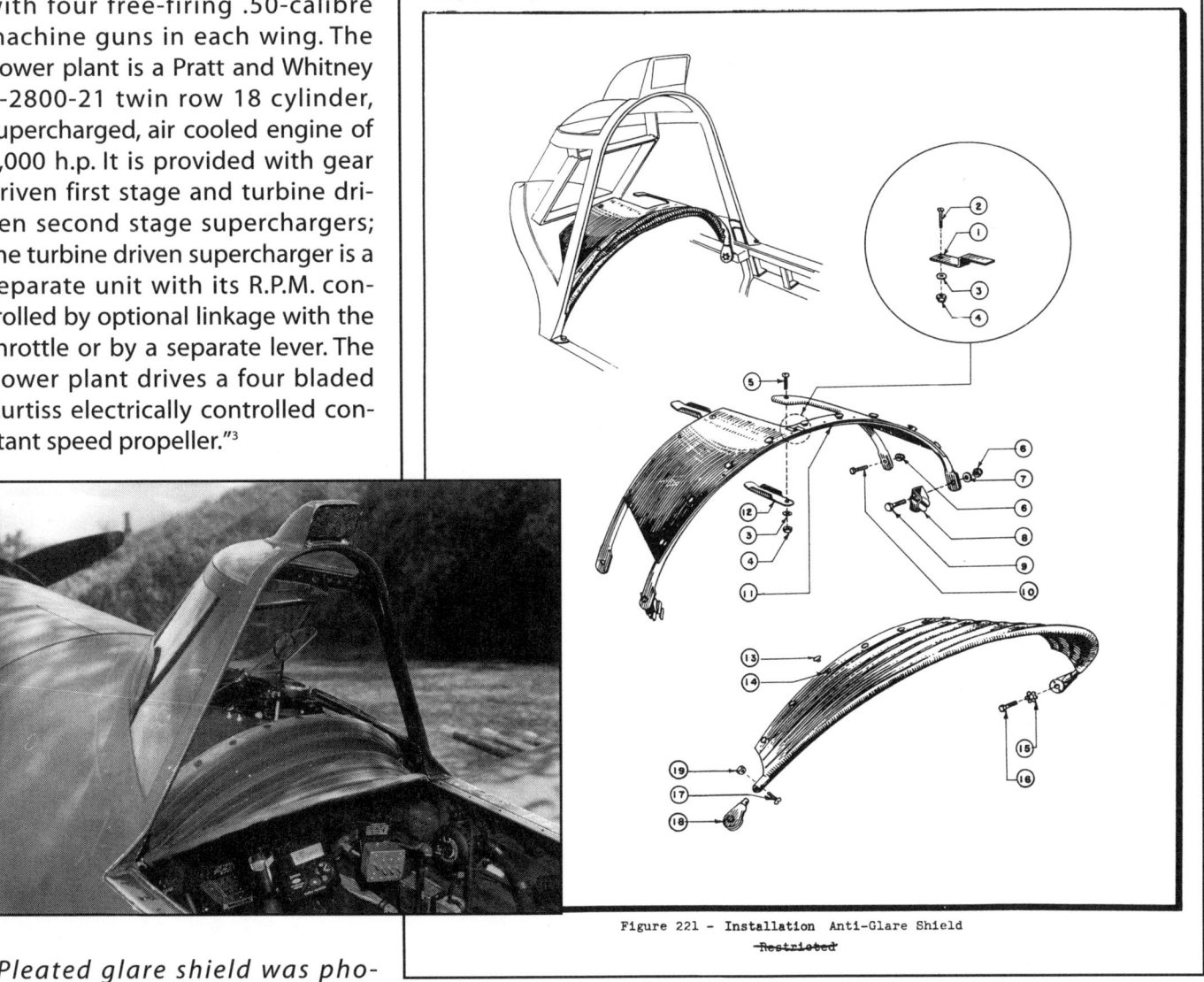

Pleated glare shield was photographed in a razorback P-47D of the 318th Fighter Group. (Tom Foote Collection)

Fixed and pleated P-47D glare shield sections permitted instrument-panel visibility in adverse lighting conditions. (AAF)

Early P-47B showed transition from XP-47B's elliptical aft fuselage windows to angled canopy framing. With dice painted on the cowling, this Thunderbolt featured a temporary sign proclaiming: "Lucky Seven! Gift of the Republic Aviation Employees." (Bodie/SDAM)

doors force the gear into the locked and down mode. In flight, the P-47C canopy could be opened. At high speeds, "it is necessary to pull the small ring on the right forward side of the canopy releasing spoiler flaps to assist in sliding the canopy back," the AAF evaluation explained. If the P-47C flipped onto its back on the ground, thereby jamming the canopy, "it is possible to remove the side panels from either the outside or inside of the cockpit, enabling an average-sized pilot to get out of the cockpit."[4]

A defining edition of the Thunderbolt was the P-47D, which underwent a remarkable evolution in its production life without changing its suffix letter. Early D-models were similar to P-47Cs; the adoption of R-2800-59 engines and water injection pushed speed well over 430 miles an hour. During production of D-models, underwing pylons were added for bombs or drop tanks. Most radical of all, a bubble canopy and new windscreen design replaced the familiar razorback, while the model still remained P-47D. Wider paddle-blade propellers introduced during P-47D production further enhanced performance. Production of P-47Ds numbered 6,315 aircraft; to reach this tally, a second assembly line was set up in Evansville, Indiana.

The sole XP-47E was a conversion from the last P-47B (41-6065), fitted with a pressurized cockpit. Another B-model (41-5938) tested

The XP-47B used elliptical aft cabin windows to provide a slim measure of view to the aft quarters for detection of other aircraft. Intercooler doors cut into the Thunderbolt's fuselage sides. (Lin Hendrix via SDAM)

Stateside P-47D-RE (42-22261) showed heavy use of scalloped dark green camouflage paint blotches to break up angularity of olive drab vertical fin and rudder. (AAF via McChord Air Museum)

laminar flow wings under the designation XP-47F.

Curtiss-Wright entered Thunderbolt production with the completion of 354 P-47Gs, essentially similar to D-models.

The two XP-47Hs were testbeds for a 2,500-horsepower Chrysler 16-cylinder liquid-cooled engine. The suffix letter "I" was not used to identify any AAF aircraft models to avoid confusion with the number "1".

The single XP-47J (43-46952) was an experiment in performance upgrades that led to a top speed of 504 miles an hour claimed by Republic in August 1944. Changes included deletion of a pair of the .50-caliber machine guns, and relocation of the turbosupercharger inlet farther aft.

The XP-47K was a converted D-model that introduced the bubble canopy in July 1943. The XP-47L (42-76614) was essentially a D-model with greater fuselage gasoline tankage, up from 305 gallons to 370 gallons.[5]

To counter the threat of fast German jet and rocket aircraft, an interim answer was found in the 130 P-47Ms fitted with R-2800-57 engines and CH-5 turbosuperchargers for speeds of 470 miles an hour at 30,000 feet.

The last production model of the Thunderbolt, the P-47N, was devised with long Pacific missions

The P-47K introduced bubble canopies to the Thunderbolt series, fashioned after a British design. (Republic)

in mind, as the AAF practiced a form of selective mutation for aircraft to be delivered to diverse fighting fronts. Big difference between the P-47N and the previous M-model was an 18-inch increase in wingspan of the P-47N. The N-model's larger wing was also strengthened to take two 93-gallon gasoline tanks internally in addition to underwing drop tanks as well as a 100-gallon centerline tank.

Republic constructed 1,667 P-47Ns at Farmingdale, Long Island, New York, plus 149 at Evansville, Indiana, before the end of the war prompted cancellation of thousands more. Final deliveries of Farmingdale N-models were completed in December 1945, closing out a Thunderbolt production run of 15,683 aircraft, making the P-47 the most-produced American fighter in history.[6]

Following a visit by AAF officials at Republic's Farmingdale, Long Island, plant in 1944, the prototype N-model was described. The wing-stub addition "required a redesign of the ailerons for better roll characteristics, (and) the final modification has resulted in better roll characteristics for the N than for the earlier models." The AAF paper continued: "No radical sacrifice in flying or performance characteristics are apparent. A slight reduction in the rate of climb is expected. The level flight speed remains unchanged, dive and zoom unchanged, rate of roll improved. This has all been possible due to the fact that the new (R-2800) C engine has an additional 200 H.P."[7]

When the prototype P-47N was being tested in 1944, the need was envisioned for this fighter to escort B-29s on Pacific raids at an altitude of 30,000 feet. The fuel-laden N-model was forecast to be able to escort B-29s at that high altitude, perform 20 minutes of combat, and return with a fuel reserve of 30 minutes, on a mission with a radius of 1,300 miles, lasting more than 12 hours.[8] (Later, Gen. Curtis LeMay would boldly take the B-29s down to low altitudes at night over Japan

The XP-47J (43-46952) topped out at around 500 miles an hour. It featured a modified razorback canopy which promised better visibility for the pilot. Armament was reduced to six .50-caliber machine guns to reduce weight. (AAF/SDAM)

Bullet-nosed XP-47H (42-23297) tested an experimental Chrysler V-16 engine that ultimately joined other reciprocating powerplants on the scrap heap in the wake of the dawning turbojet era. At 38 feet, four inches, the H-model was the longest Thunderbolt by more than two feet. (AAF/SDAM)

to increase accuracy. But the P-47Ns reaching the Pacific did not want for combat; their range and combat load was employed in a variety of ways.)

The AAF personnel evaluating the potential of the P-47N in 1944 said runway length for the laden Thunderbolts "will hardly be a problem due to the fact that the N will usually be based with the [B-]29s where 10,000 feet will be the usual length." The AAF paper reported on a Republic test pilot's observations about the long duration prospects for P-47N sorties: "Pilots will have to be selected for aggressiveness, stamina, and of the 'non-sweating-out' type."[9]

Some Fliers Weary of Increased Range

As greater fuel capacity stretched the range of P-47s to enable them to reach out on long missions, some pilots found the experience debilitating. A veteran Pacific fighter pilot who had flown P-38s, P-39s, P-40s, and P-47s told an AAF debriefer in early May 1945: "We liked the P-47, but it is not built for long range operations. The problem of sheer physical fatigue is too great. I well remember one mission, covering better than 1700 miles, which kept us out eight hours, 15 minutes. We carried three drop tanks and jettisoned them after four hours. By using very low power settings, three of our flight just managed to make it back to the base. The fourth ran out of gas 10 minutes from home, and ditched his plane very smoothly. He got out, but the Japanese picked him up before our air-sea rescue could take over."[10]

The Thunderbolt pilot who related that episode said: "As a flight leader, I am definitely opposed to running such long-range missions in P-47s. The cockpit is too small for comfort, and there is just no way to relax. Such missions should be scheduled only when it is a case of extreme necessity against a very important target." The pilot, who had a total of 625 hours in a

Sole XP-47E was modified from the last P-47B. Nonstandard cabin was pressurized on the E-model. (Republic)

variety of fighters, said: "From our experience, I would say that it will be absolutely necessary, in the event long-range fighters are to be used in the Pacific, to provide more comfort for the pilot. They cannot otherwise stand up under this physical grind."[11]

Chrysler-Powered XP-47H Faded

As early as 1942, the Chrysler company was developing an inverted V-16 liquid-cooled engine intended for aircraft. Known as the XI-2220, the engine needed an aerial testbed. Although the AAF's Materiel Command said the Chrysler powerplant required a purpose-built airframe to make optimum use of the V-16's potential, this would delay testing of the engine. Therefore, the big P-47 was deemed a suitable host for the engine. First considered for installation in a P-47B in 1942, the project did not move to that stage until 1944, when a P-47D-15 was modified for the purpose. Prior to that time, Republic's commitments for development and production of other P-47 models for the AAF had to take priority. By August 1943, Chrysler was given the go-ahead to mount their V-16 in a P-47. Interest in the sometimes-shunted project gained more momentum in the spring of 1944 when the engine proved its ability to deliver 2,500 horsepower.[12]

The XI-2220 engine's crankshaft was divided by a gear to turn the propeller shaft. The engine weighed nine-tenths of a pound for every horsepower it could produce. Chrysler used a crankshaft, heads, and other parts that were built to

Extended canopy allowed student and instructor to fly in the TP-47G, which had reduced fuel capacity as a result. In addition to a pair of official TP-47Gs, some other field-modified Thunderbolts accommodated two people. (SDAM)

greater strength than this engine configuration required, to allow for the possibility of future development of even more horsepower. For the XP-47H, a Curtiss Electric propeller was the logical choice because the XI-2220s had not been built with provision for running an oil line through the propeller shaft, as required by hydraulically-operated propellers. Here, too, the Chrysler program faced wartime priorities that substituted a lesser propeller for the model that would have best capitalized on the engine's capabilities because the desired Curtiss Electric prop variant was in high demand for another fighter project.[13]

To convert the P-47D-15 into XP-47H configuration necessitated complete redesign of the airplane from the firewall forward, including cowling, engine controls, fuel and oil system, exhaust manifold and shrouds, and a stout engine mount. A new belly cowl and exhaust ducts aft of the firewall, plus ducting for the liquid-coolant system, also was required. The redesign also accommodated a CH5 turbosupercharger. According to an AAF report on the project, "No changes were made that affected fuselage structural members."[14]

The XP-47H, modified by Chrysler and Republic at Republic's facility in Evansville, Indiana, first took to the air on 27 July 1945, with a takeoff gross weight of 13,427 pounds. An AAF performance chart placed the XP-47H at a maximum speed of 414 miles an hour at 2,500 horsepower, at 30,000 feet and a design gross weight of 15,138 pounds.[15]

About 18 hours of flight tests had been completed when the propeller shaft failed during the 27th flight of the XP-47H in November, forcing an uneventful deadstick landing. The Chrysler engine exhibited some teething problems — not surprising for a new, complex 16-cylinder piece of high-performance hardware. Noted was a surge in manifold pressure at altitude. An AAF summary of the project laconically noted: "It was decided to install the remaining engine in the second airplane for delivery to Wright Field but because of the lack of interest in the project and since there was no longer any requirement for the airplane or engine, this airplane was ferried to Freeman Field, Indiana, for disposition."[16] The juggernaut Chrysler V-16 reciprocating aircraft engine reached for performance, but was overtaken by the burgeoning jet age.

XP-47J in Detail

The XP-47J was intended to improve performance of the P-47 by use of new engine accessories and propeller assemblies along with a weight-reduction program. Ultimately, the future of the J-model dimmed as engineers were needed for another Republic fighter venture, the XP-72. An AAF report on the J-model explained: "…it was decided that production possibilities were remote and therefore work should be continued on a limited basis only with a view to obtaining all performance necessary from one flight article."[17]

By November 1942, Republic engineers and AAF representatives agreed on the basic ratio-

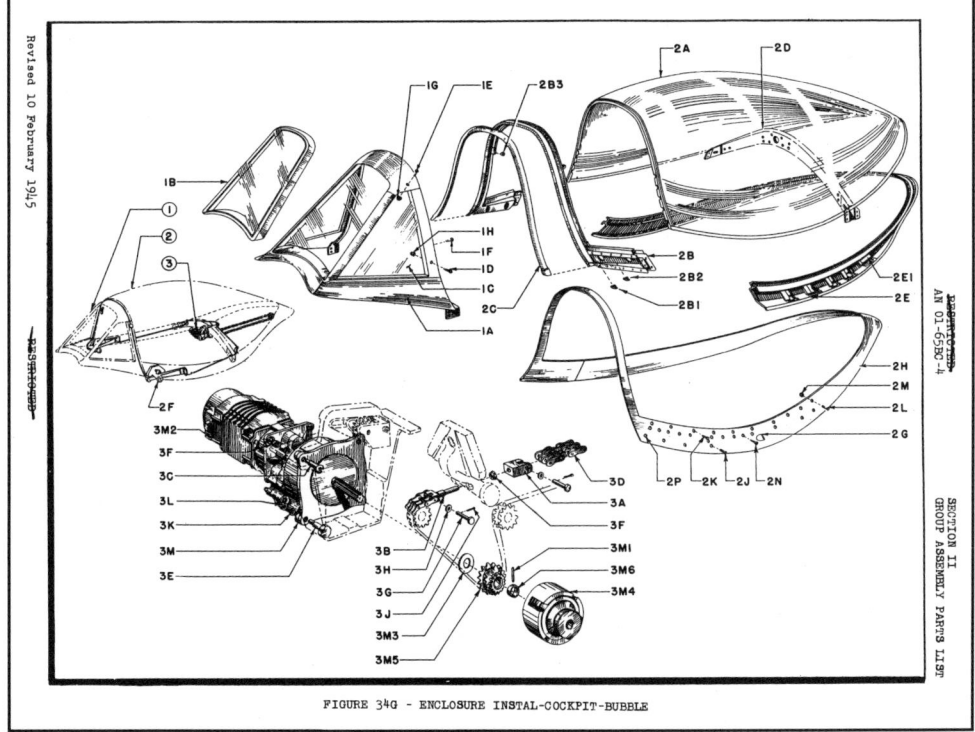

Mechanically-actuated bubble canopy for P-47s mated to a revised windscreen that presented a flat slab of armor glass to the front instead of the v-shaped windscreen of razorback Thunderbolts. (Drawing used in Thunderbolt parts book AN 01-65BC-4)

Big-winged P-47N with squared tips was last production Thunderbolt variant. Extended anti-glare panel behind bubble canopy is evident in low head-on view. Dorsal antenna mast is slightly offset from fuselage centerline. Flown at Wright Field during the war, this N-model bore the nickname "The Repulsive Thunder Box". (Gene Furnish)

nale for the XP-47J, which included an improved R-2800 engine with water injection and fan cooling; a new propeller; a new General Electric turbosupercharger with a higher critical altitude, and mounted farther forward than on previous Thunderbolts; the use of only six .50-caliber machine guns, limited to 267 rounds per gun; deletion of the rear gas tank; and a reduction in radio gear. Other changes were subsequently suggested. As codified in January 1943, the XP-47J program was intended to wring out the maximum performance possible from the Thunderbolt.[18]

The XP-47J required about 70 percent new production tooling to accommodate all of its changes from previous Thunderbolts. While the prospects for the J-model looked good, the AAF insisted that its eventual mass production could not be made at the expense of a gap in producing Thunderbolts of any model. Consideration was given to introducing J-model attributes one at a time on the assembly line, if the XP-47J warranted such. Republic warned that some slow-down in production was inevitable.

Even as the J-model was evolving on paper and on the shop floor, changes were forthcoming that caused construction slippages. As early as April 1943, selection of a new Aeroproducts contra-rotating propeller was made for the XP-47J. A month later, Republic was instructed to put a free-blown bubble canopy on the second of two flight-worthy J-models then on order. (Ultimately only one P-47J was completed.) As the J-model progressed, it became apparent to Republic that this was no longer a worked-over P-47D, and cost overruns mounted as the company undertook essentially a redesign of the whole airplane. Accordingly, the AAF authorized a payment to Republic of more than $458,000 to cover the unexpected costs.[19]

Tests of contra-rotating propellers made by Curtiss and Aeroproducts were performed using a P-47D, and results did not show marked improvement over the simpler single propeller. Some hope remained that the J-model's anticipated engine improvements would capitalize on the contra-rotating propellers, but in March 1944, Pratt and Whitney said problems in perfecting the engine/propeller combination warranted dropping the contra-rotating propeller from the P-47J program. Using a new 13-foot diameter Curtiss propeller, Republic claimed a top speed of 505 miles

Razorback P-47D number 42-76298 became a hangarless queen, its bent Curtiss Electric prop blades graphically telegraphing its metamorphosis from flying machine to spare parts source. The presence of full wrap-around invasion stripes suggests the belly landing took place between 6 June and sometime in July 1944. Smooth-jacketed M-2 machine guns rested against the wing/fuselage juncture as usable parts continued to breathe life into other Thunderbolts. Missing is the pointed, streamlined Curtiss Electric prop dome, revealing the prop pitch mechanism. (AAF)

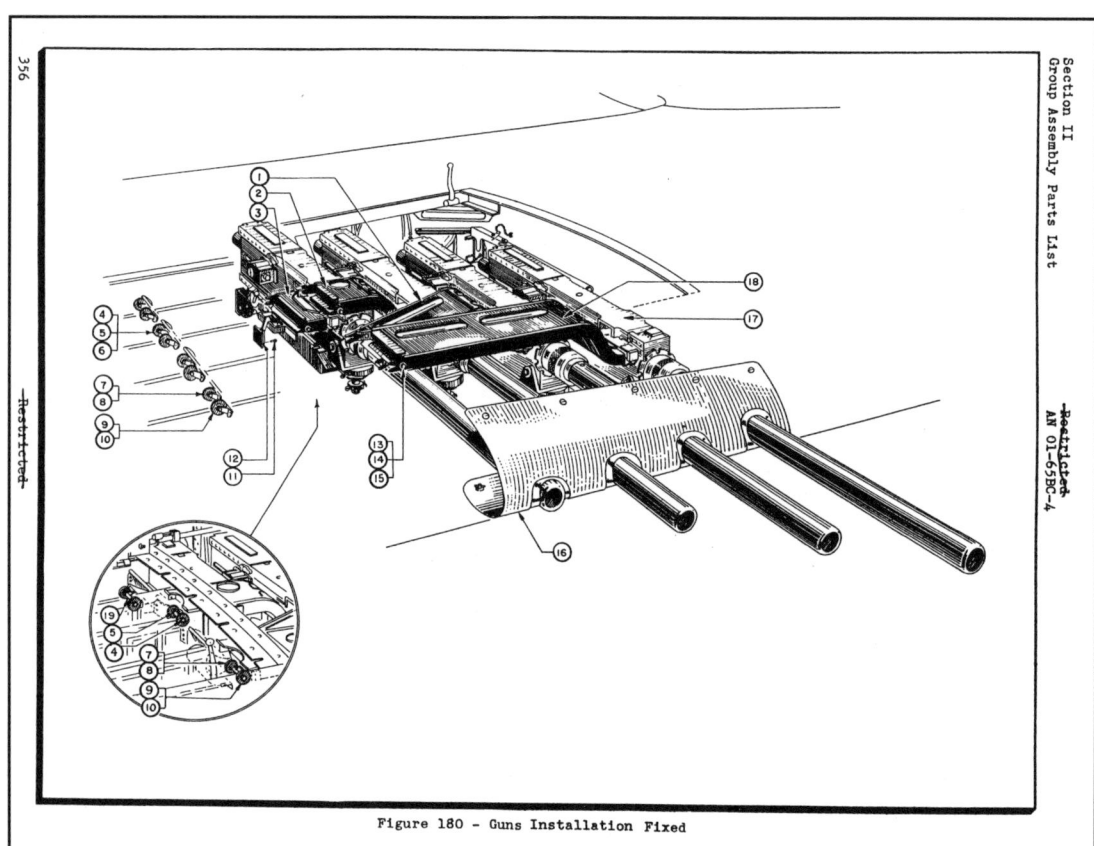

Smooth metal jackets encased the barrels of P-47 .50-caliber machine guns, as depicted in a wartime drawing of the right wing installation. Rollers (part numbers 4 though 10 in the drawing) helped feed linked ammunition from hoppers outboard of the guns. Rigid feed chutes (parts 1, 2, 3, and 18 in the drawing) helped carry ammunition to each gun. (AAF)

A natural metal finish bubble-top P-47D, with cuffed Curtiss Electric propeller, gleamed beneath a photographer's sky at the Republic factory. Stagger of guns, necessary for ammunition feed, is readily evident. (Republic via USAFM)

an hour on 5 August 1944. Subsequent Army Air Forces tests in 1945 could only verify a computed speed of 493 miles an hour at 35,000 feet — still no mean feat. (Cruise speed of the testbed XP-47J was touted in one report to be 400 miles an hour.)[20]

If the XP-47J faded in the shadow of the promising XP-72, both lost the race to the new breed of turbojet fighters then taking form.

During the Air Force's high-speed flight tests of the XP-47J, failure of the exhaust manifold system at 36,000 feet brought an investigation. An AAF report said the cause of the failure "was attributed to the fact that the original exhaust system was inadequate to accommodate the increased power of the engine (2800 h.p.) plus the fact that a larger capacity supercharger had been installed and the supercharger exhaust had been constricted to take advantage of the jet thrust available in the exhaust gases, all of which created much higher back pressure and temperature than the

Armorers carefully placed linked .50-caliber ammunition in the wing of Lt. Col. Francis Gabreski's victory-decorated P-47D in England in 1944. Large ammunition access cover hinged to the rear. Top covers of two of the machine guns are open for loading, visible as vertical black parts protruding up from gun bay. (AAF)

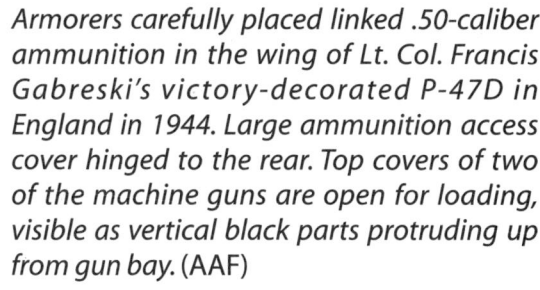

Four rows of partitioned ammunition compartments are visible in the left wing of a Thunderbolt in England. (AAF)

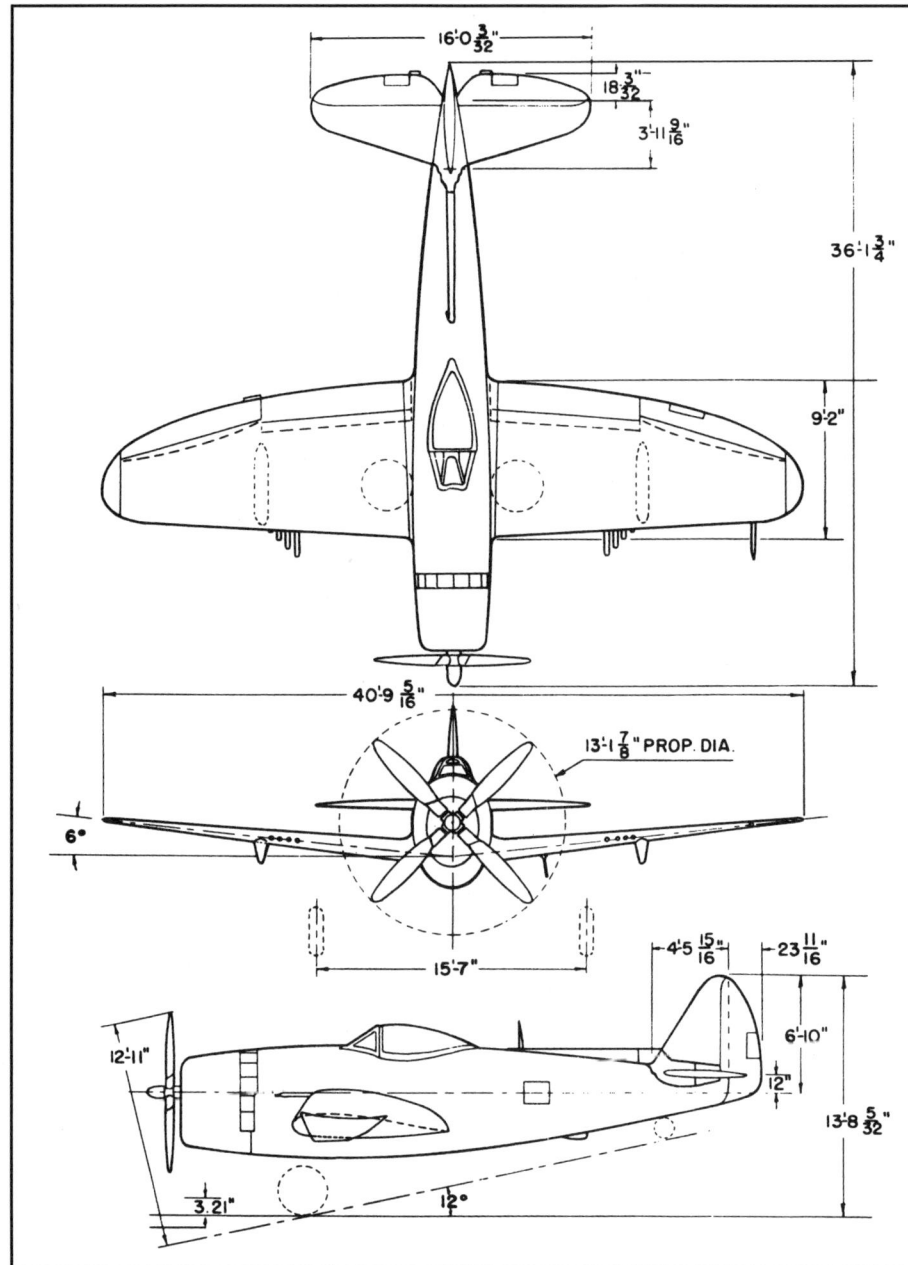

A Republic Aviation three-view drawing depicts salient aspects of the P-47D-30, including the addition of a dorsal fin for added stability following the cut-down of the rear fuselage from previous razorback variants. The Dash-30 model was fitted with dive flaps to help relax the grip of compressibility in high-speed dives. (Republic/SDAM)

exhaust system could accommodate." The AAF never flew the XP-47J at maximum power.[21]

An Arsenal of Thunderbolts

More than 15,500 Thunderbolts were built, tallying the largest quantity of any American fighter. (Sources vary from a 1945 AAF tally of 15,585 P-47s, to other counts nearly a hundred aircraft higher.) As Thunderbolt production accelerated, predictably, unit costs diminished. Up through 1941, the cost of a P-47 was put at $113,246. In 1942, this dropped to $105,594; by 1943 it averaged $104,258. For 1944, the unit price of a Thunderbolt was $85,578, and the following and final year of production, P-47 costs reached their lowest, averaging $83,001.[22]

The price of a P-51 Mustang dropped from $58,698 in 1942 to $50,985 by 1945; in the last year of P-40 production (1944), they averaged only $44,892 each. The production volume and longevity of the Thunderbolt owed something to the aircraft's demonstrated capabilities, and not to its bottom line.

Though the first flight of the XP-47B preceded America's entry into World War Two by more than a half-year, only one P-47 was listed on AAF rolls until March 1942 when the tally bumped up to three aircraft. By May of that year, five P-47s were on hand in the AAF, and, as production gained momentum, this jumped to 30 Thunderbolts in June 1942, 59 by July, and 120 by August. In May 1943, the AAF P-47 tally exceeded 1,000 Thunderbolts. High point in AAF Thunderbolts on hand was reached in May and June of 1945, when Air Force statisticians counted 5,595 P-47s in their service.[23]

By the end of 1943, the AAF had 1,514 P-47s arrayed against Germany; in the Pacific by that December, 391 Thunderbolts were in the various theaters of operations versus Japan. The pipeline of aircraft from the United States continued to rush fighters to the fronts, so that by April 1945, as the European war was drawing to a close, the AAF listed 2,355 P-47s in the fight against Germany. By August 1945, in the various Pacific theaters, the Japanese faced a total of 1,329 AAF Thunderbolts.

P-47 MODEL CHARACTERISTICS

MODEL	SPAN / LENGTH	GROSS WEIGHT	TOP SPEED
XP-47B	40 ft. 9 in. / 35 ft. 5 in.	12,086 lbs.	412 mph at 25,800 ft.
P-47B	40 ft. 9 in. / 35 ft. 5 in.	12,245 lbs.	429 mph at 27,800 ft.
P-47C	40 ft. 9 in. / 36 ft. 1 in.	13,500 lbs.	420 mph at 30,000 ft.
P-47D-11	40 ft. 9 in. / 36 ft. 1 in.	13,500 lbs.	433 mph at 30,000 ft.
P-47D-25	40 ft. 9 in. / 36 ft. 1 in.	14,500 lbs.	428 mph at 30,000 ft.
XP-47H	40 ft. 9 in. / 38 ft. 4 in.	14,010 lbs.	414 mph at 30,000 ft.
XP-47J	40 ft. 11 in. / 33 ft. 3 in.	12,400 lbs.	507 mph at 34,300 ft.
P-47M	40 ft. 9 in. / 36 ft. 4 in.	13,275 lbs.	473 mph at 32,000 ft.
P-47N-1	42 ft. 7 in. / 36 ft. 1 in.	16,300 lbs.	467 mph at 32,500 ft.[25]

With caveats for variations in sources of data, and differences in actual performance under combat versus possibly-stereotyped test performance, a compendium of Thunderbolt statistics shows trends in the development of the P-47 series. Weights for the P-47 sometimes exceeded the listed gross, reaching a maximum of 20,700 pounds for the P-47N. Top speed for the XP-47J was reported by Republic (some sources put it at 504 or 505 mph), but not attained in AAF testing.

From 1942 through 1945, the accident rate for P-47s in the continental United States averaged 127 per 100,000 flying hours. Of frontline AAF fighters, only the P-51 was lower, with an averaged rate of 105 accidents of all types per 100,000 flying hours. And yet, so many P-47s were flown stateside that the total number of Thunderbolts wrecked in crashes in the U.S. was 1,125 aircraft between 1942 and 1945, compared with only 358 P-51s in that time span, and 758 P-38s. The statistics are sobering: in a full-tilt race to field high-performance fighters, the exigencies of war led to higher mishaps than in recent memory. In 1944, 474 P-47s were listed by the AAF as "wrecked" in stateside accidents — far more than one a day![24]

The P-47 had some things in its favor. Its wide landing gear stance made the Thunderbolt less prone

Short-bodied P-47B lacked engine mount extension of later models, placing oil cooler vent on lower cowling closer to wing leading edge than on subsequent Thunderbolts. (Hendrix/SDAM)

to the groundlooping that plagued some new pilots in narrow-tracked P-40 Warhawks. And the Thunderbolt's rugged structure (one wag called it an airborne fox hole) served to protect both airplane and pilot in off-airport landings.

NACA Tested Thunderbolts

The National Advisory Committee for Aeronautics (NACA), forerunner of NASA, evaluated Thunderbolts. The NACA was charged with helping American manufacturers improve efficiency and performance of their designs, a calling that took on patriotic urgency once America entered the war. (One listing shows "XP-47" undergoing a drag reduction program at the NACA laboratories at Langley Field in Virginia in May 1940, suggesting even the unbuilt lightweight Allison engine aircraft originally designated XP-47 may have been evaluated by the NACA. Some tests were at the request of the AAF for specific problems; others may have been more exploratory.[26]

Between March and October 1942, the NACA at Langley used P-47B number 41-5897. P-47B 41-5901 was carried on the NACA Langley records between July and October 1942. Two P-47Cs, including aircraft 41-6102, were assigned to NACA Langley from October to December 1942. P-47C-1 number 41-6130 arrived in October 1942 and remained on hand until August 1944. The XP-47F (41-5938) was at Langley between February and October 1943. P-47D-3-RE number 42-8207 was on the NACA Langley records between October 1943 and March 1944. A P-47D-15-RA (serial not listed) arrived in July 1944 and departed 12 months later. P-47D-28-RE number 42-28541 also went on the NACA Langley records in July 1944, but remained listed there until April 1948, long after the end of the war. Long-wing P-47N-1-RE 44-87790 was carried by NACA Langley from January to July 1945. P-47D-30-RA number 44-33441 was at Langley for NACA duties from January 1945 to October 1948. P-47N-25-RE 44-89303 arrived in August 1945 as the war was ending, and did not leave until December 1950, the last Thunderbolt to depart NACA Langley.[27]

[1] Gordon Swanborough and Peter M. Bowers, *United States Military Aircraft Since 1908*, Putnam, London, 1971. [2] "Tactical Employment Trials on the Republic Airplane P-47C," Report of the Army Air Forces Board, AAFSAT, Orlando, Florida, 16 February 1943. [3] *Ibid*. [4] *Ibid*. [5] Ray Wagner, *American Combat Planes*, Doubleday, Garden City, New York, 1968. [6] Ray Wagner, *American Combat Planes*, Third Edition, Doubleday, Garden City, New York, 1982. [7] AAF paper, "Facts Gathered at the Republic Plant at Farmingdale Relative to the P-47N," Tactical Bombardment Section, circa April 1944. [8] *Ibid*. [9] *Ibid*. [10] Memo, Subject: "Operations — P-47," by Capt. W.H. Strand, published by Air Intelligence Contact Unit, HQ, AAF Redistribution Station No. 3, Santa Monica, California, 4 May 1945. [11] *Ibid*. [12] *Army Air Forces Technical Report No. 5601*, "Final Report of Development, Procurement and Acceptance of the XP-47H Airplane," by A.K. Dillon, 1 July 1947. [13] *Ibid*. [14] *Ibid*. [15] *Ibid*. [16] *Ibid*. [17] *Army Air Forces Technical Report No. 5504*, "Final Report of the Development, Testing, and Acceptance of the Republic XP-47J Airplane," by Capt. George D. Coichagoff, 26 June 1946. [18] *Ibid*. [19] *Ibid*. [20] *Ibid*. [21] *Ibid*. [22] *Army Air Forces Statistical Digest, World War II*, Office of Statistical Control, HQ, USAAF, December 1945. [23] *Ibid*. [24] *Ibid*. [25] Ray Wagner, *American Combat Planes*, Third Edition, Doubleday, Garden City, New York, 1982. [26] James R. Hansen, *Engineer in Charge — A History of the Langley Aeronautical Laboratory, 1917-1958*, National Aeronautics and Space Administration, Washington, D.C., 1987. [27] *Ibid*.

Head-on view of a Thunderbolt probably depicts a P-47C; this model introduced capability to carry drop tank or bomb on centerline shackle. (SDAM)

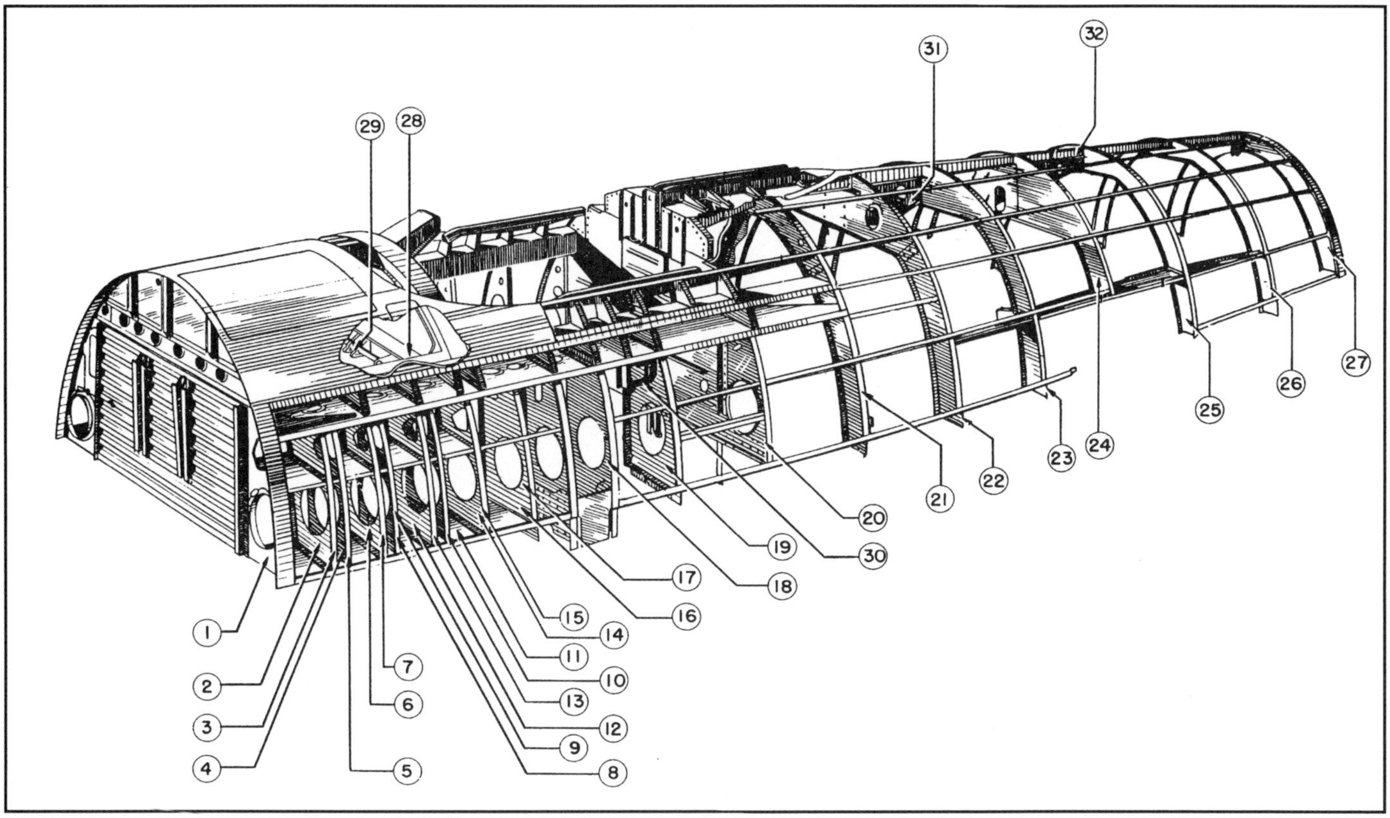

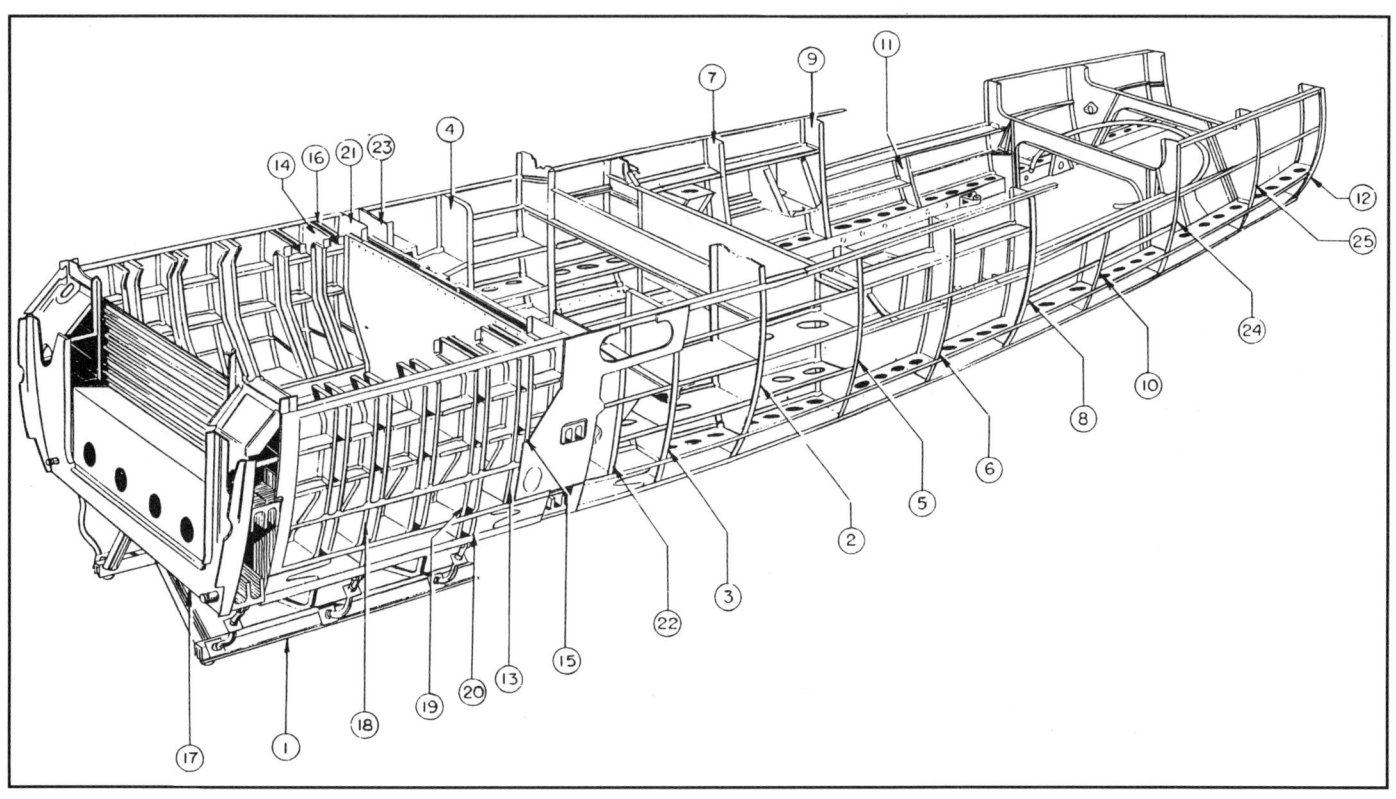

Some fighters of the era were assembled as top and bottom halves. Shown is the structure for the top half of a bubble-top Thunderbolt, with an opening for the single cockpit, as depicted in a Dash-4 parts book. (AAF)

Lower half of a Thunderbolt fuselage structure includes belly landing skid structure (part number 1). (AAF)

REPUBLIC P-47 THUNDERBOLT

Employees pushed the 10,000th Thunderbolt through a paper banner in ceremonies at the Republic plant in September 1944. This aircraft subsequently served in Italy. (Gen. Oliver Echols Collection)

~~RESTRICTED~~
AN 01-65BC-4A

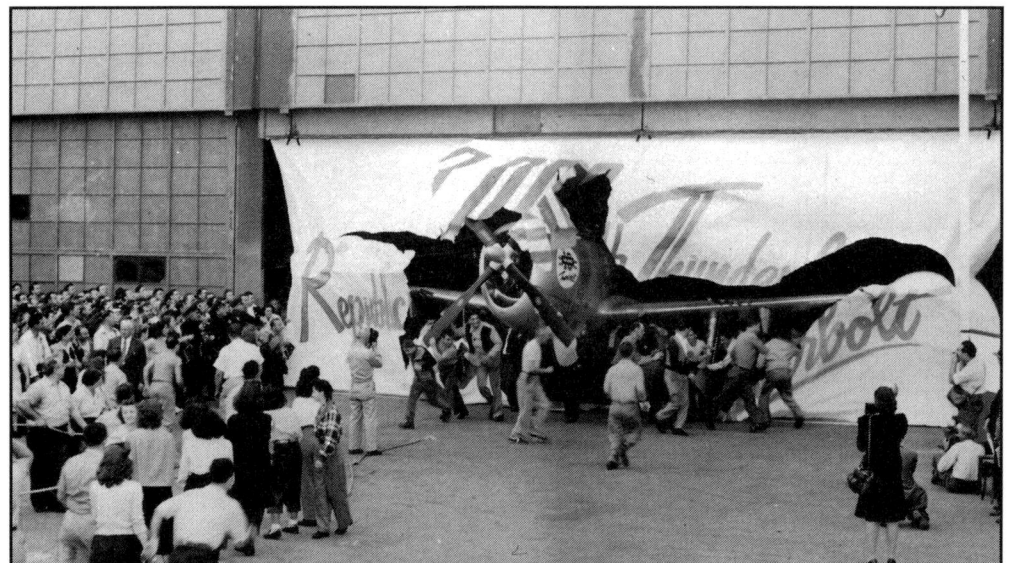

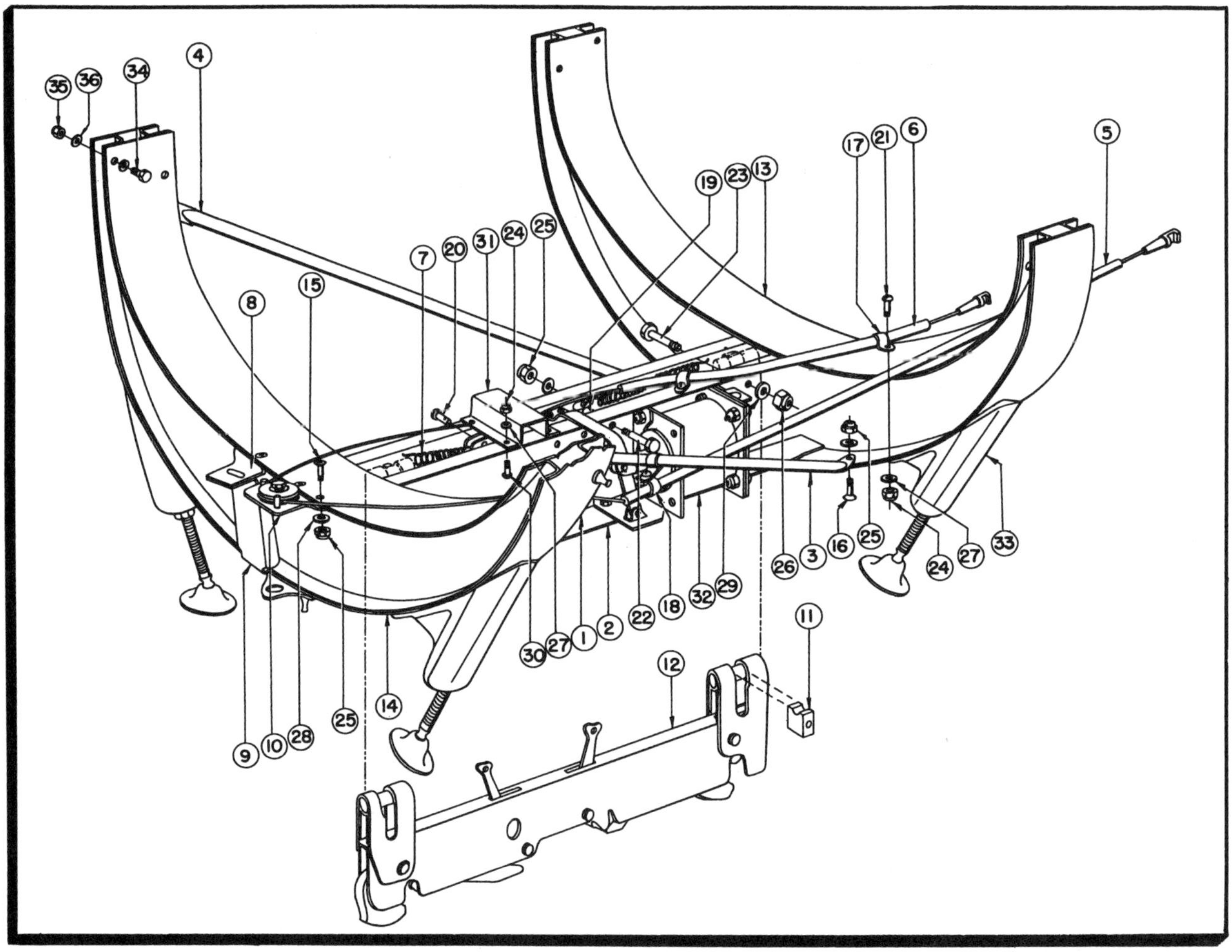

~~RESTRICTED~~

Section II
Group Assembly Parts List

Figure 133 - Support Instal - Belly Tank

Support structure was introduced to carry a centerline tank, using a standard B-10 bomb shackle (part 12 in the technical-manual drawing). Four sway braces (part 33 in the drawing) had screws with pads that could be adjusted to keep a drop tank or bomb snug and free from side-to-side movement.(AAF)

Line art from a P-47 illustrated parts book shows the built-up structure of the landing gear doors, with a cutout in the lower door (number 2 in the drawing) to accommodate the strut. Fuselage-mounted doors (number 1 in the drawing) were built as robustly as the main doors. (AAF)

Section II
Group Assembly Parts List

~~Restricted~~
AN 01-65BC-4

Figure 113 - Fairing Installation Landing Gear
~~Restricted~~

P-47 main landing gear doors attached to the strut in two pieces. When weight on the wheels compressed the landing gear oleo strut, the lower door slipped behind the upper door. Beefy doors attached to the fuselage completed the enclosure in flight. On this jacked example, weight is off the wheel, allowing the strut and lower door to extend downward. (U.S. Air Force)

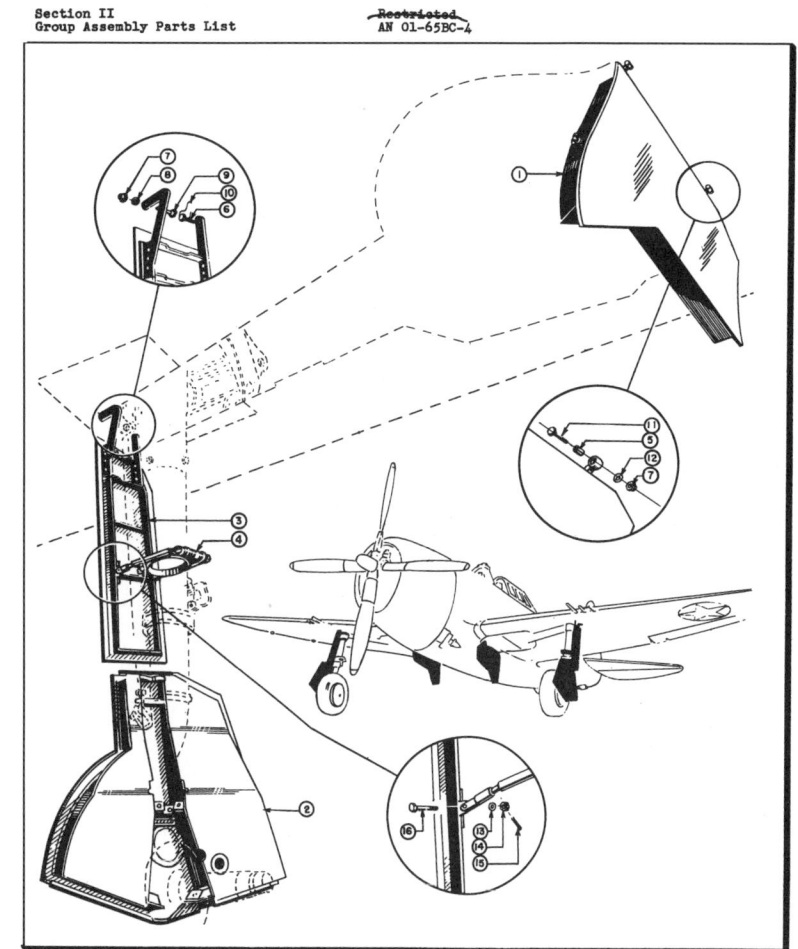

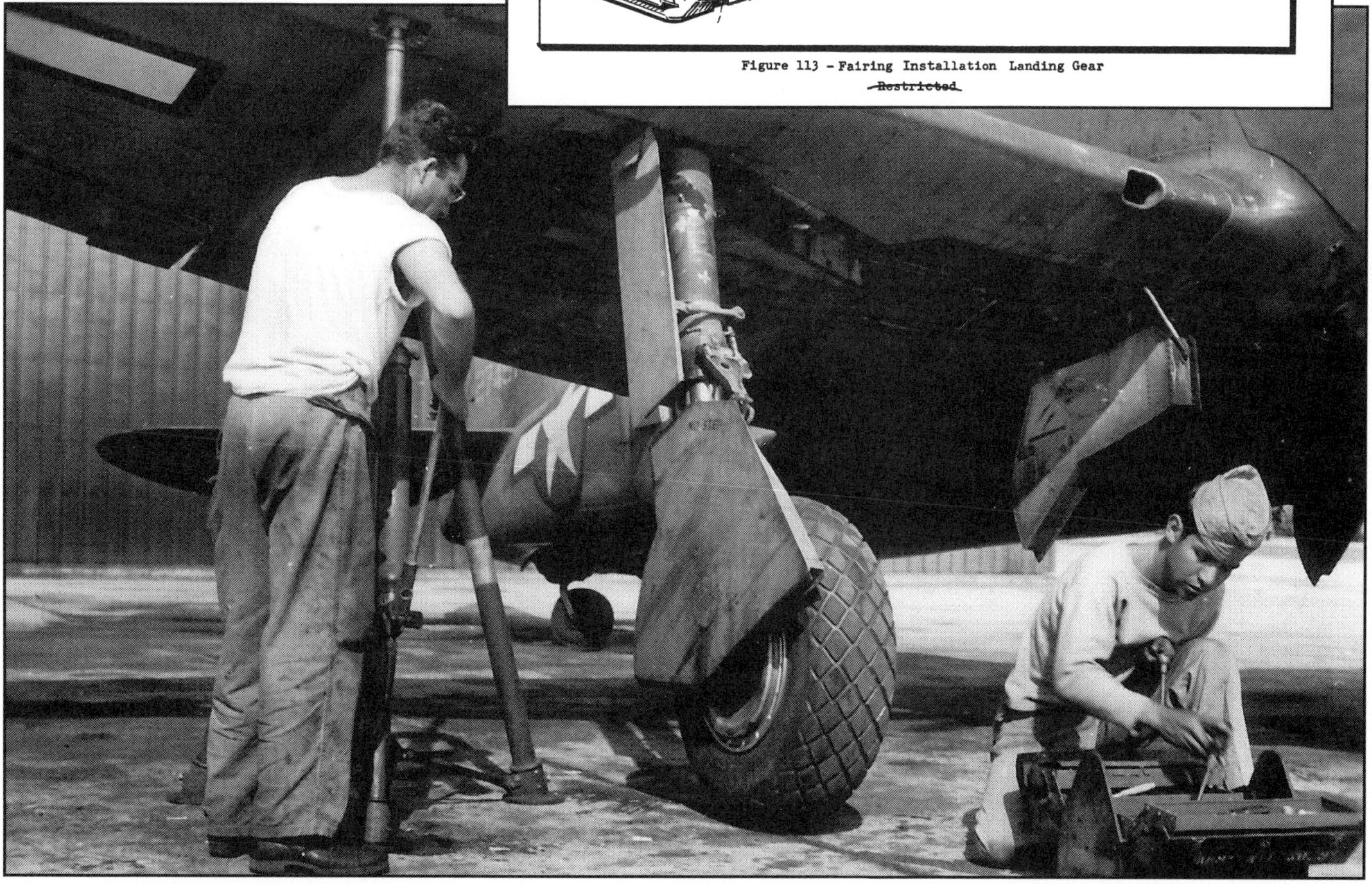

Battle damage photo of P-47D number 42-8614's instrument panel, taken 8 October 1943, showed the placement of an optimistic 700-mile-an-hour airspeed indicator, located beneath placard of safe indicated diving speeds that admonished: "For dive recovery apply power – never reduce power." (AAF)

The left cockpit sidewall of P-47D-5 (42-22534) held fixtures including the levers of the mixture, propeller, and throttle quadrant; flap and landing gear controls, and intercooler shutter control. Photo taken 7 September 1943. (AAF)

Section II
Group Assembly Parts List

AN 01-65BC-4

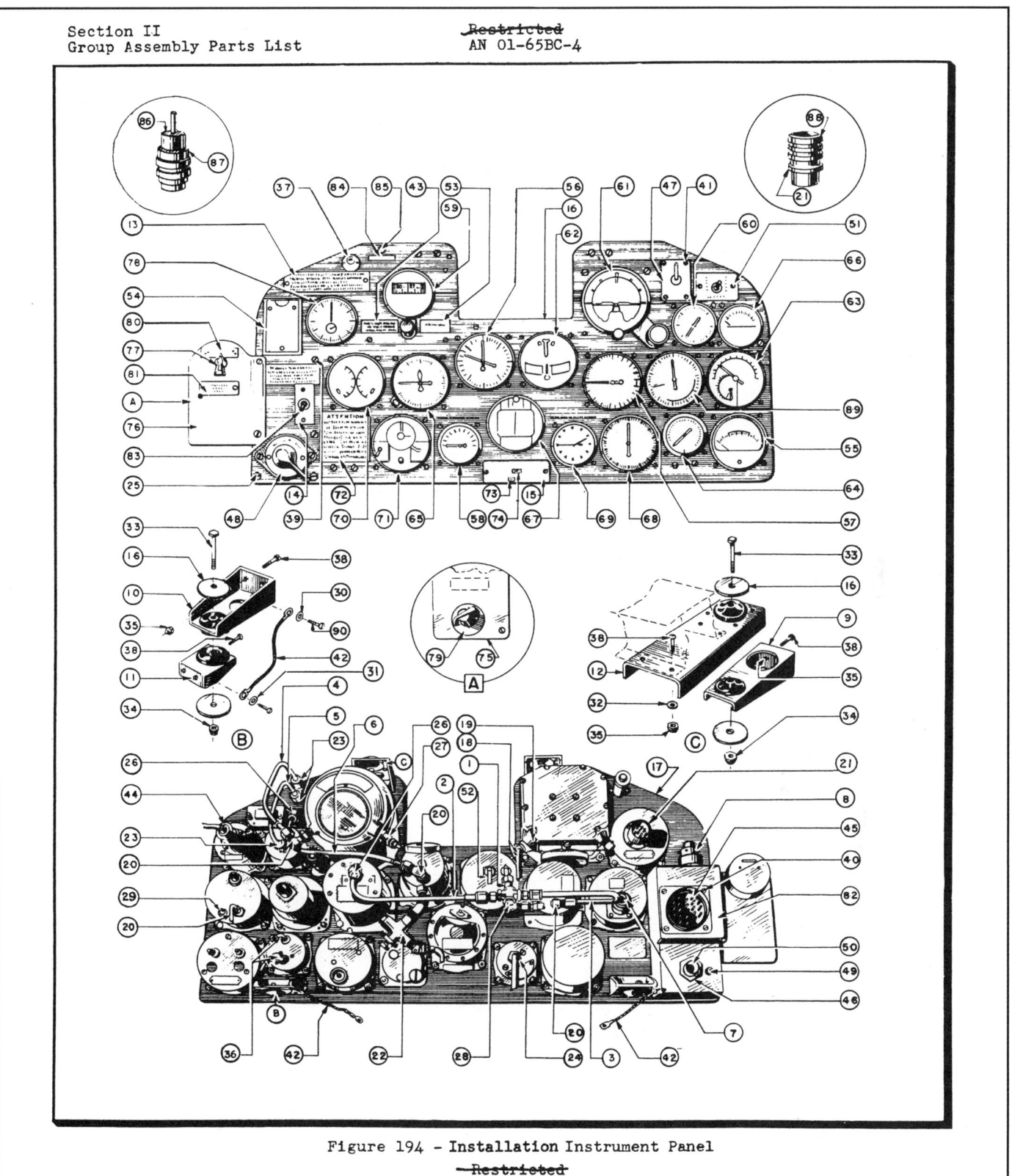

Figure 194 - **Installation** Instrument Panel

Variations in instrument panel layouts were not unusual on World War Two aircraft. The version depicted in this drawing from a P-47 illustrated parts book placed the altimeter in the location indicated by number 65 on the drawing. The airspeed indicator is number 56. Number 61 is a Type C7 artificial horizon. Instrument number 67 is a Type B16 compass. Part 48 is an A9 ignition switch. (AAF)

REPUBLIC P-47 THUNDERBOLT

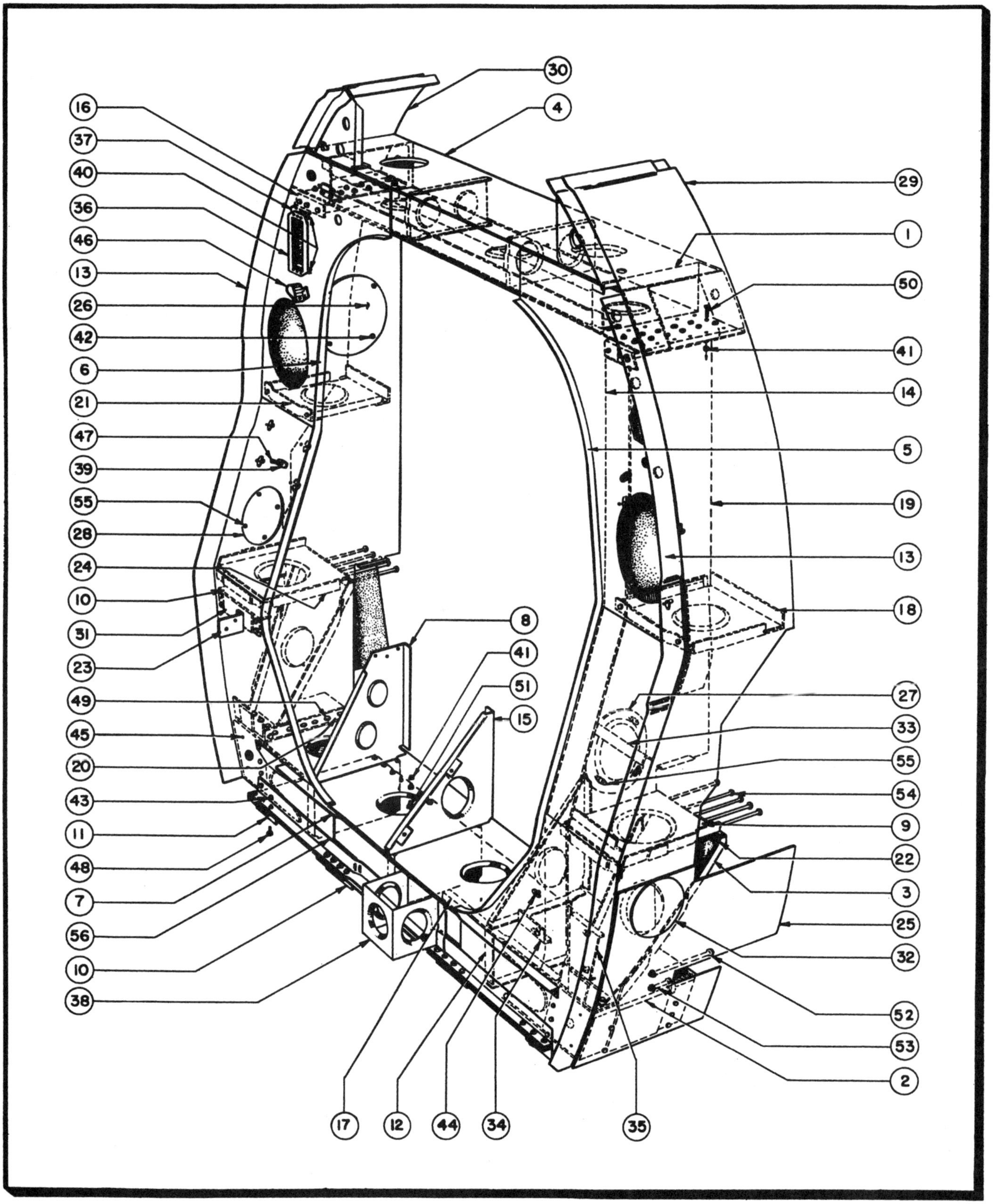

Section II
Group Assembly Parts List

AN 01-65BC-4A

Firewall extension benefited balance of P-47Cs and later variants. (AAF)

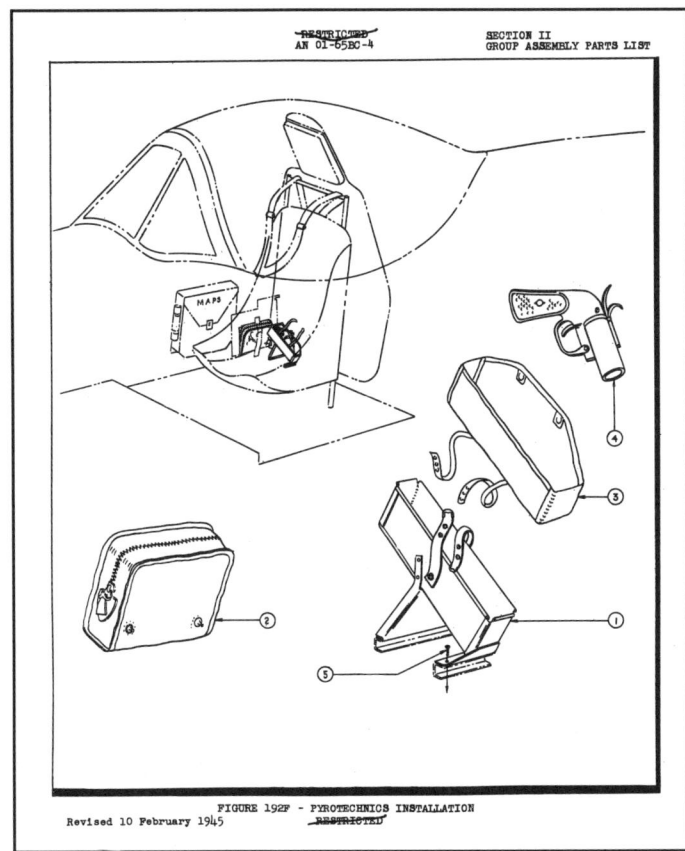

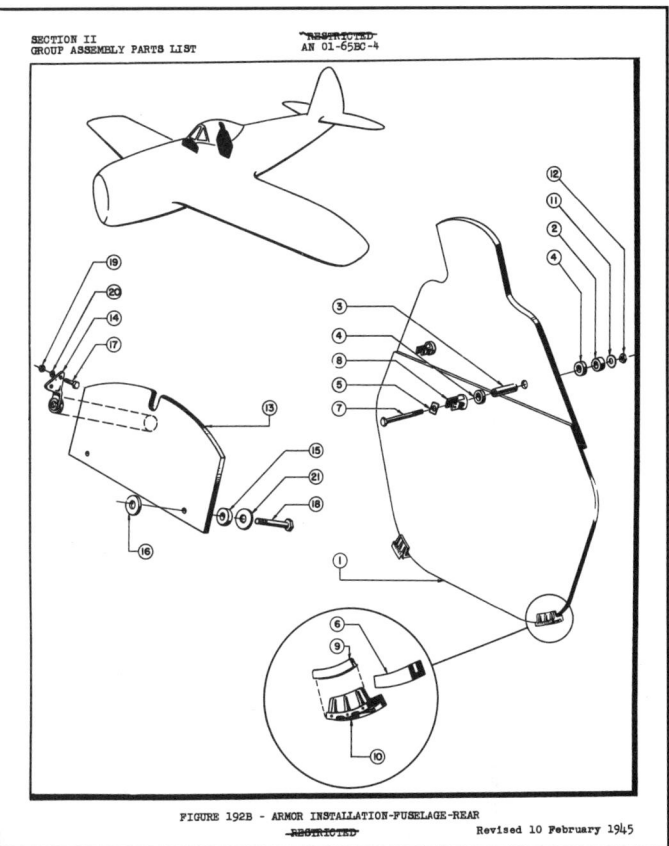

Parts-manual art shows stowage of a signal flare gun and associated equipment in a bubble-top Thunderbolt. (AAF)

Below: *Silver razorback P-47D of the 354th Fighter Group, Ninth Air Force, was modified with British-designed Malcolm hood, a bulged plastic canopy that improved visibility. (Barrett Tillman Collection)*

Above: *Bubble-top P-47M and P-47N armor plate array included a very important seat back and headrest protection of steel, as well as a frontal plate ahead of the instrument panel. The beefy R-2800 engine provided a measure of frontal protection as well! (Artwork from AN 01-65BC-4 P-47 illustrated parts book)*

One of the early P-47Cs (41-6584) taken into combat by Eighth Air Force came to rest with all four prop blades neatly kinked on 29 November 1943. The tailwheel remained extended, but the mains are nowhere to be seen. White tail stripes on vertical and horizontal surfaces were intended to help identify and distinguish P-47s from Luftwaffe FW-190s. (U.S. Air Force)

A hole in the left stabilizer big enough to stand in could not down this 318th Fighter Group P-47D pilot in the Pacific. (Tom Foote Collection)

The Battle is Joined

Thunderbolts in Combat

The Thunderbolt entered combat on 8 April 1943 as Eighth Air Force squadrons of the Fourth, 56th, and 78th Fighter Groups took C-models over the Continent. AAF and Republic specialists pored over early Thunderbolt combat reports in an effort to judge the P-47's strengths and weaknesses. Its literal strength — an incredible ability to absorb battle damage — was evident early on. Climb and maneuverability in P-47Cs needed improvement, but the big fighter dived impressively. As with all AAF fighters developed on the eve of World War Two, Thunderbolts initially suffered from lack of range — or, more to the point, if they were to figure as escort fighters over hotly-contested Germany, P-47s would need to get some more range.

Early use of belly tanks began with a mission on 28 July 1943 in which 128 P-47s, according to an AAF letter to Republic, "furnished withdrawal support as far as Cleve, for a heavy bomber mission. This was the first time that belly tanks had been used for operational purposes and their use permitted deep penetration of the continent to about 275 miles from base. The fighters were successful in driving off from 50 to 60 enemy aircraft which were attacking our bombers, and in the encounters eight enemy aircraft were destroyed, two probably destroyed and five damaged for the loss of one P-47."[1]

Early P-47 escort forays with drop tanks were gratifying. On 17 August 1943, 276 belly-tank equipped Thunderbolts operated in three waves to give support to two heavy bomber formations that attacked targets in Germany. According to an AAF letter describing the action: "The two (bomber) formations were furnished support as far as Eupen, about 265 miles from base. Withdrawal support was furnished one formation at the same point. On meeting the returning force, the P-47s found the bombers under attack of 50 to 60 enemy fighters. The tactics of the P-47s, remaining

Two P-47s of the 56th Fighter Group's 61st Squadron (HV-W, Little Butch, a D-model and HV-E, Francy Ann, P-47C number 41-6265) nearly mask another P-47D as the three Thunderbolts taxi in England in 1943. (Fred LePage Collection)

above the bombers and diving over them to break up head-on attacks, were successful. In the encounters our fighter claims were 20 enemy aircraft destroyed, three probably destroyed, and three damaged for a loss of three P-47s."[2]

Belly tanks enabled Eighth Air Force P-47s to escort B-17s all the way to Germany for the first time on 27 September 1943, as the heavy bombers used radar to hit the port of Emden.[3]

Thunderbolts from Eighth Air Force inaugurated bombing operations on 25 November 1943 with a pair of unusual attacks. The 353rd Fighter Group dispatched more than 50 P-47s, 16 of which each carried a 500-pound bomb. They approached an airfield at St. Omer at 15,000 feet, diving to release their bombs through flak at 8,000 to 10,000 feet. Fourteen of the Thunderbolts actually bombed, but a disappointing three hits on the airfield were all that could be tallied. Meanwhile, the 56th Fighter Group placed 50 P-47s laden with one 500-pound bomb apiece behind a B-24 Liberator, whose bombardier was to acquire the enemy airfield and bomb at the proper moment, with the Jug pilots releasing their bombs when they saw bombs drop from the B-24, at 24,000 feet. The plan went astray when a malfunction delayed the Liberator's bomb release, causing most of the Thunderbolts' bombs to fall beyond the airfield. The idea of using single-engine fighters in high-altitude bombing formations had appeal because the fighters could become defenders once their bomb was dropped. It also afforded the Eighth Air Force a way to spread over more targets, diluting the Luftwaffe. However, once sufficient aircraft of all kinds were on hand for the Eighth Air Force, the use of fighters as formation bombers was an inefficiency.

In the Pacific, Thunderbolts wrote headlines as well. On 5 November 1943, Fifth Air Force P-47s engaged Japanese fighters over Wewak in a gun battle for which the Thunderbolt pilots claimed about 20 enemy airplanes downed. On several occasions, Fifth AF P-47s ranged over Wewak, drawing out Japanese fighters for a number of fights as 1943 waned. On 17 December 1943, Fifth Air Force Thunderbolts raced to the aid of Allied forces on the Arawe peninsula who were under attack by 35-40 Japanese warplanes. The P-47 fliers claimed at least 10 victories that day.[4]

Tactical Trials of the P-47C

Before the first Thunderbolt unleashed eight .50-calibers in combat, the AAF evaluated the P-47C in a series of tactical employment trials that pointed up strengths and weaknesses. Results of the trials were published in a formerly-Confidential report dated 16 February 1943. One problem com-

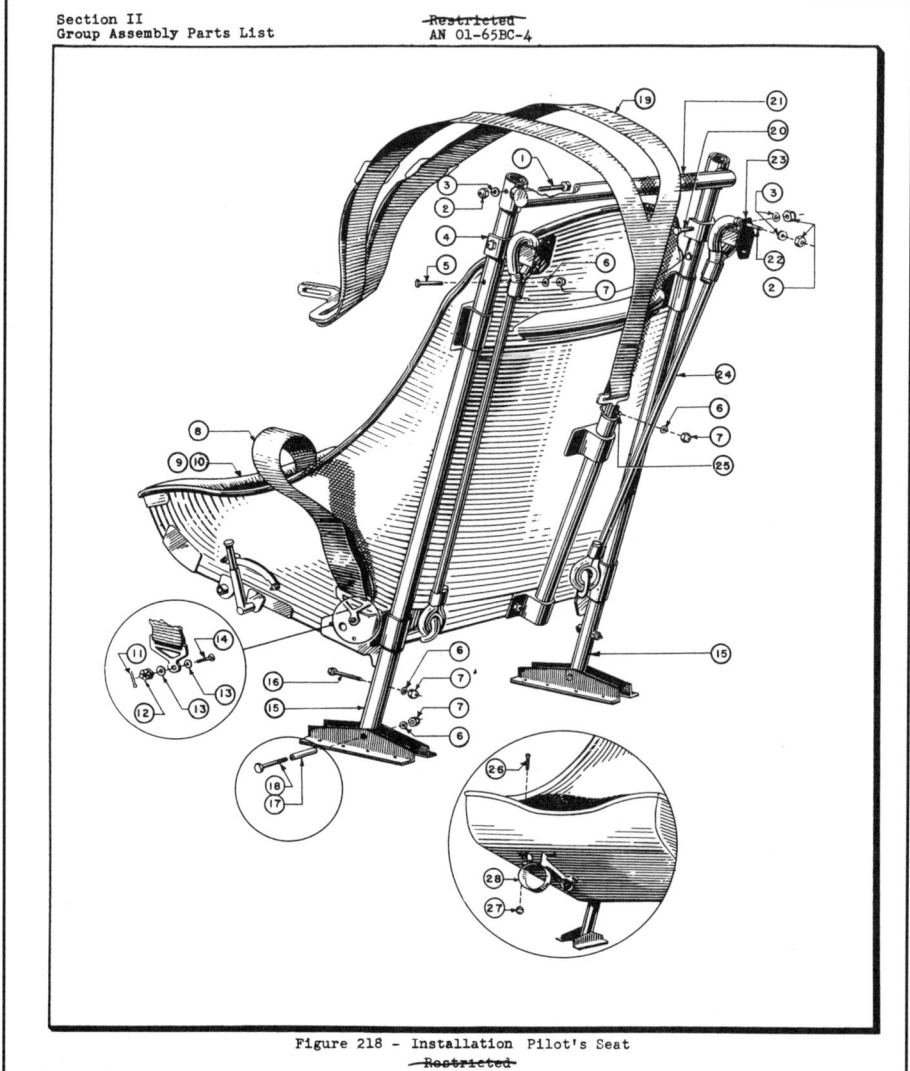

P-47 pilot's seat typical of C- and D-models included shoulder harness (number 19 in line art).(AAF)

Two P-47Cs and three P-47Ds of the 56th Fighter Group's 62nd Fighter Squadron show their 1943 markings, including yellow rings around the fuselage star insignia (but not the wing insignia), and white tail and nose bands for quick identification markings to distinguish the P-47 from the FW-190. P-47C LM-O (41-6347) has early-style comic strip Lil' Abner cartoon art. (Fred LePage Collection)

mon to many fighters was the intrusion of nose contours in the pilot's forward vision. The AAF tactical trials report on the P-47C noted that the sighting view over the nose was limited to about 3-1/2 degrees, which reduced deflection shooting to small angles only.[5]

This highlighted the salient problem facing fighter pilots. Unless they were attacking from dead astern or head-on, it was necessary for fighter pilots to aim ahead of the current location of the intended quarry to ensure the path of the bullets would intercept where the enemy airplane would be at the time of impact. Sometimes, to achieve the correct amount of deflection for such a shot, the firing fighter's nose obscured the target aircraft as the firing aircraft had to pull hard to aim at the expected path of the target aircraft. The AAF report said, "it is impossible to hit a target flying over 115 mph when the P-47 is firing from a vertical bank from 90 degrees to the target. It would be necessary to limit an attack to approximately 20 degrees to hit a 300 mph target."[6] The war of the World War Two fighter was clearly a tail-chasing event.

The AAF evaluators said all eight guns worked satisfactorily, "apart from occasional stoppages." Muzzle flash at night — not the P-47's normal operating environment — "is found to be bright enough to spoil the pilot's vision for a short period," the report noted. The P-47C could carry 425 rounds for each machine gun, but ammunition belts had to be carefully loaded any time more than 275 rounds per gun were to be carried, or stoppages were likely to occur. At 275 rounds, the continuous fire time lasted only 20 seconds; with 425 rounds, the total duration of fire was about 30 seconds.⁷ (Short bursts were generally used in combat with M-2 aircraft-type .50-caliber machine guns, to conserve ammunition and keep from overheating the guns.) To keep the guns from freezing at high altitude, hot air was piped from the exhaust collector ring to the wings, with a cockpit control allowing the pilot to select gun heat as needed.

The AAF tactical evaluation found big nose of the P-47 a hindrance to taxiing: "The lack of forward visibility of the P-47 on the ground definitely limits its taxiing speed. The nose must be swung continuously from one side to the other to allow the pilot proper forward vision, thereby necessitating extremely slow taxiing."⁸ (This problem was common to most tailwheeled fighters of the war; sometimes a spotter would ride the wing of a fighter to enable faster taxiing.)

Takeoff in the P-47C was said to be long but relatively easy. "With the tailwheel locked there is only a slight tendency for the airplane to swing to the left, and this can be countered by either rudder trimming or use of right rudder. The average take-off run, carrying combat load, is about 1,450 feet and to clear a 50-foot obstacle, about 2,230 feet." Initial climb in the P-47C was called "poor" in the tactical evaluation. (Coupled with its cumbersome taxiing traits, the slow climb suggested the P-47 was not destined to be an interceptor to be scrambled from a standing start. Its forte would be air-to-air high-altitude dogfighting and air-to-ground attack sorties.) In the air, the P-47C was praised by its AAF evaluators, who said: "The airplane, although large and heavy, handles beautifully; it is light and positive on the controls at all speeds. At no time is its great weight felt by the pilot."⁹

Stalling traits of the P-47C were considered good; a pre-stall shuddering gave the pilot warning, and there was no tendency for the aircraft to drop off on either wing. "At

By the time the 56th Fighter Group's Lil' Abner was photographed on 26 November 1943, the cartoon art had changed to a profile view, and white bars and a red surround had been added to the national insignia. (U.S. Air Force)

The lead airplane in this 1943 echelon formation of 56th Fighter Group P-47s has the 1942-early 1943 national insignia on the lower left wing; some ETO Thunderbolts carried star insignia on the bottoms of both wings instead of only the lower right as was standard. (Fred LePage Collection)

As the 62nd Fighter Squadron posed for a photo over England in 1943, their P-47Ds and Cs show a few irregularities in the size of squadron and aircraft letters applied to their fuselages. (Fred LePage Collection)

![P-47D photo]

P-47D (42-7975) of the 56th Fighter Group's 63rd Fighter Squadron in 1943; numerals 123 over intercooler door on fuselage were a vestige of Republic Aviation construction numbers that were often painted out on P-47s in service. (Fred LePage Collection)

high altitude, however, the use of too much rudder at the stall should be avoided or a spin may develop. Should this occur, the normal recovery methods will bring the airplane out without difficulty." At combat weight, the turning radius of the P-47C was large, "but this is expected in a heavy airplane with a high wing loading," the AAF evaluation noted. "At high speeds the airplane turns nicely but mushes when the turn is tightened. If the turn is tightened further, a high speed stall will occur," the evaluation explained.[10]

Landing the P-47C with an approach speed of 130 miles an hour, full flaps were recommended for the final glide to touchdown. "It is necessary to use a little power in order to keep the plugs clear," the AAF evaluation noted. (It is not uncommon to hear high-performance World War Two fighter engines popping and backfiring on approach to landing.) "The landing itself is easy and the airplane sits down in a three point position very nicely." The self-locking tailwheel fostered an easy landing roll. The evaluation said: "Brakes can be applied immediately with little fear of nosing over, but should be used sparingly to avoid damaging the tires and overheating the brakes." (This was different from some other fighters like P-36s and P-40s that nosed-up fairly easily, especially with new pilots. The wide track of the Thunderbolt's main gear also made it more resistant to ground-looping than some taildraggers.) It was necessary to unlock the tailwheel before attempting a turn on the ground, "or the tail wheel tire will be liable to rupture on attempting to turn."[11]

Razorback Thunderbolts like the P-47C used a V-shaped windscreen. "It was found while flying in rainy weather that the V-shaped windshield kept very clear," the AAF evaluation noted. The good visibility in rainy conditions was singled out as an asset during low-altitude flight.

The AAF tactical evaluation included a curiously-worded general evaluation of the P-47C that found it "inferior" to the twin-engine Lock-

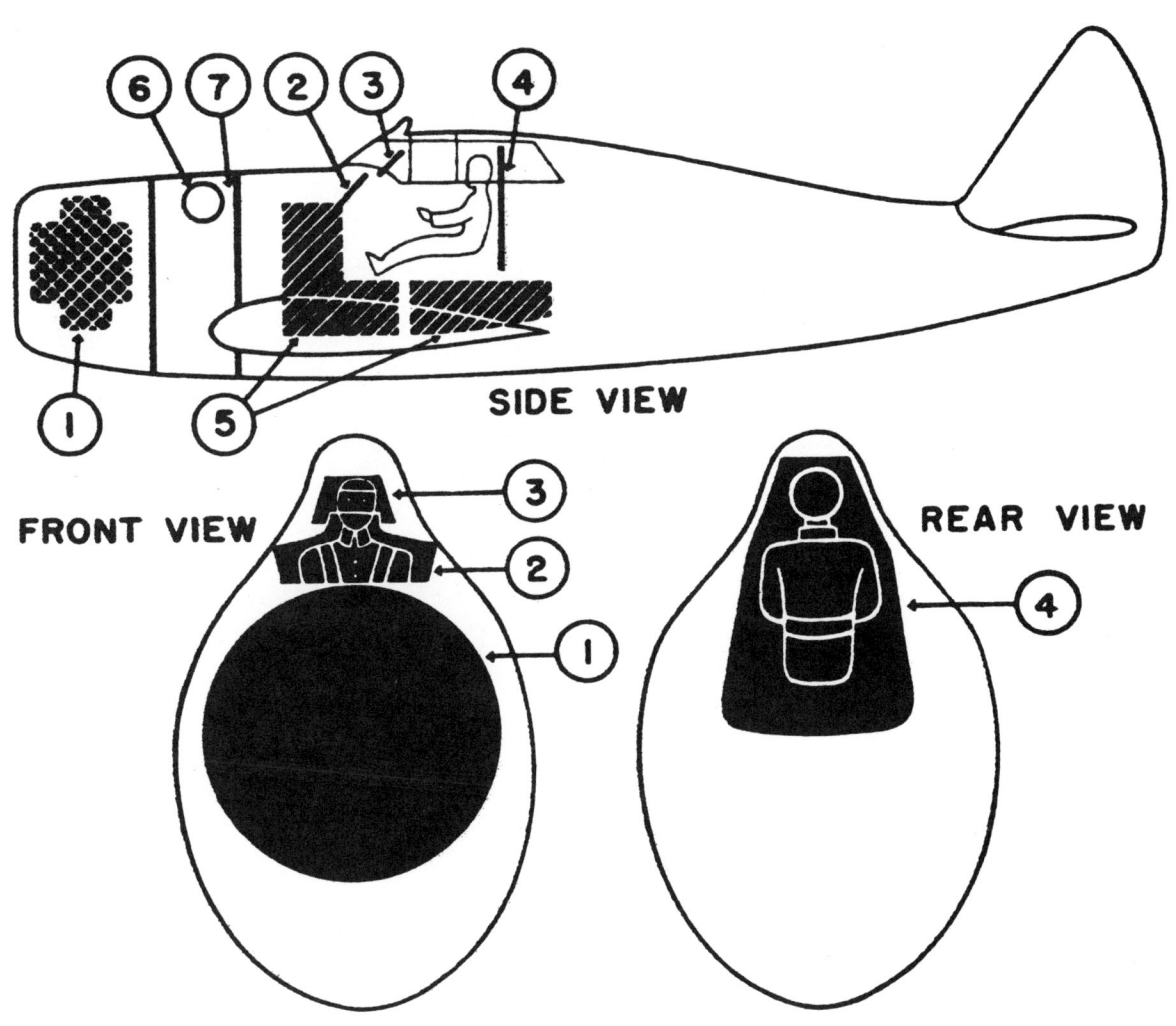

Wartime drawing depicted the degrees of protection the P-47C pilot enjoyed, both from deliberate armor plating and from other aircraft components. (AFHRA)

With German fighters on their tails, it was inevitable Thunderbolts would occasionally take hits from the rear through the arc of their massive four-blade propellers. The pilots of these two Thunderbolts were lucky; the bullets tore holes in their hollow steel Curtiss Electric prop blades, but the P-47s kept flying back to base. (U.S. Air Force)

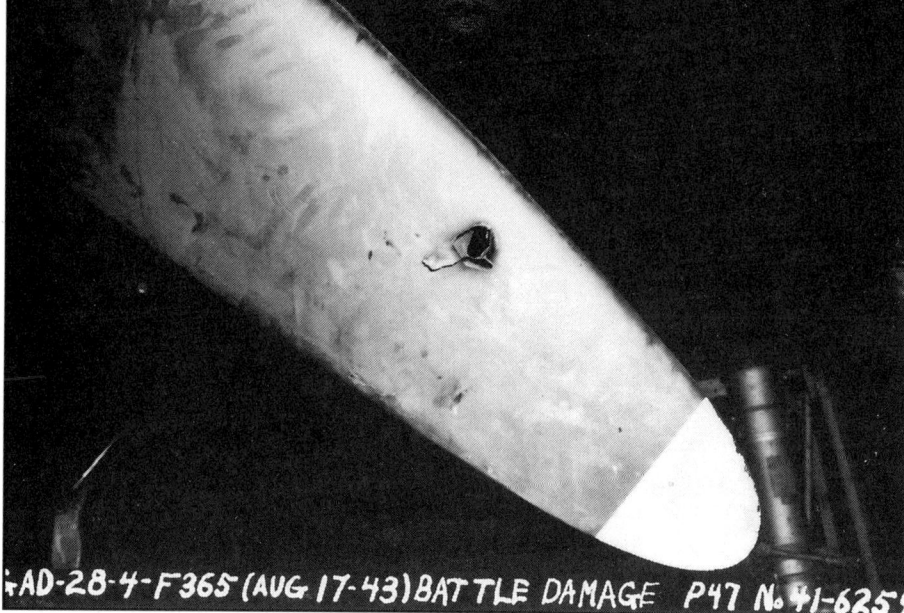

heed P-38G Lightning "in all ways except visibility, ease of flying, firepower, ease of maintenance, and a slight speed advantage." In detail, the AAF report noted: "The P-47C for tactical operations is better than the P-40s up to and including the P-40K, and the P-39s up to and including the P-39D. Due to the superior speed and firepower, and ease of maintenance of this airplane, its tactical performance is superior to the above mentioned airplanes when employed to use these factors. This airplane should be used as a hit-and-run offensive fighter where its best characteristics can be exploited to the maximum, and its inferior climb will be of the least disadvantage."[12]

Noting the P-47C's main fighting qualities "are its high speed and heavy armament," the AAF study went on to describe a phenomenon not frequently discussed in the literature of World War Two, but which became a serious air traffic problem in later years — wake turbulence. "The P-47 also has a strong slipstream which on occasion throws an attacking airplane completely out of control," the report said. The AAF found the P-47 to be in its element between 20,000 and 30,000 feet, explaining: "When the P-47 is cruising at high speed it has an excellent chance of catching most present-day fighters and its high speed also makes it difficult to catch in level flight." If challenged by an opponent flying at a higher altitude, the Thunderbolt's best ploy was to dive away, the report said. "This maneuver would have to be very carefully executed as at present, the diving limitations which are in effect at these altitudes are easy to exceed."[13]

While acknowledging the P-47C's good roll rate, the AAF study did not recommend "that the P-47 attempt to mix it up with enemy fighters, as its turning circle is too large. The recommended tactics to adopt when attacking an enemy airplane are to deliver an attack at high speed and then break away downwards or in the opposite direction of the enemy line of flight as quickly as possible." While zoom-climbing back to altitude gave the P-47 a boost, as the momentum of the zoom wore off, the P-47C's acknowledged poor rate of climb returned.

The AAF's early tests pitted a P-47C against a P-38 in mock combat at altitudes between 10,000-15,000 feet, and again at altitudes between 25,000-30,000 feet. At the lower altitudes, the AAF study documented: "When the P-38 turned to the right, it was possible for the P-47 to follow and get in a short burst before being out-turned." The P-47 pilot was urged to break off combat before any turning engagement could get the better of him. At the higher altitudes tested, the P-47 was able to stay on the tail of the P-38 during the turning maneuvers. The report concluded: "The P-47 has a slight speed superiority at this altitude and can break off combat at will either by [a] diving turn or simply a level turn and full speed in the opposite direction. Great caution must be used to avoid over-revving the turbo. Constant glancing at the turbo tachometer in its poor location detracts the pilot's attention from the continual search required in combat."[14]

The pre-combat evaluation of the P-47C said it should not be used as a close-escort fighter because staying close to bombers at slow speeds and medium altitudes would rob the Thunderbolt of its combat strengths. "However," the report noted, "it is excellent for high top cover and escort cover, when used within its fuel range." (Subsequent developments in drop tanks, pylons, and internal tankage would increase the escort range of later model Thunderbolts.)

The AAF report found the P-47C "easier to work on than the P-38, P-39, or P-40, as most parts are easily accessible, and in general, its maintenance requirements are less demanding. Therefore the maintenance time required for comparable jobs is appreciably lowered."

Transitioning new pilots into the P-47 was forecast to be "practical and easy to accomplish." The AAF study of the P-47C said prospective pilots should be given a check ride in an advanced trainer to ascertain the pilot's grasp of necessary technique. The pilot should pass a cockpit check of the P-47,

A silver pressed paper drop tank enhanced the range of P-47D 42-75037, parked near a supply of drop tanks in protective wrappers in England on 14 January 1944. (U.S. Air Force)

and observe as many takeoffs and landings by experienced P-47 pilots as possible. The study urged: "Every effort should be made to have the pilot overcome any idea that the P-47 is 'big' and 'too much of an airplane.'"[15]

Report from North Africa

Joseph F.B. Parker was Republic's chief test pilot when he accompanied a batch of P-47s delivered to the 325th Fighter Group in North Africa in the fall of 1943. The more than 60 Thunderbolts arrived as shipboard deck loads, and consisted of some P-47D-6s and more P-47D-10s. Some of the Republic and Pratt and Whitney service representatives accompanying Parker and the Thunderbolts were still learning about the aircraft, Parker's report said, noting, in their defense, "they were damn good boys. Worked like the devil from sun up to sun down. The mistakes were very small but discouraging when working against time."[16]

Pilot Parker found some of the available technical orders out of date when he and the Thunderbolts reached Africa, so he literally rewrote portions of them, especially covering installation of belly tank capability. Once the new P-47s were ready, Parker took each of 30 pilots up in two-ship elements "for the primary purpose of introducing them to near-compressibility dives and demonstrating methods of recovering from dives whose speed approaches or reaches compressibility," a company technical report explained. "Some of the boys got into compressibility inadvertently, and this 'scared the devil out of them.' All of these group pilots fully realize what compressibility is."[17]

The batch of P-47s in North Africa made use of A-13 turbosupercharger regulators from B-24s, which were found to be "very satisfactory," according to test pilot Parker's report to Republic Aviation. When some of the Thunderbolts in the group experienced battery box explosions because of clogged bat-

Even the big, steady Thunderbolt could stand on its chin, or in this case, on a propeller blade speared into the turf. Normal white tail band and cowl edge have been overpainted. Bar under aircraft letter Z suggests this is not the first aircraft assigned to the 63rd Fighter Squadron to carry Z as an identifier. (AFHRA)

A 56th Fighter Group razorback Thunderbolt, its flaps partly extended, rested on a beach near a lighthouse following a successful emergency landing. The aircraft lacks white recognition stripes. (AAF)

tery drains, Parker's crew experimented by venting the battery with tubing leading to a grommet in the cowling. "This seemed very satisfactory although acid-proof paint was used in the immediate vicinity of the exit," Parker explained. A local hazard was rough landing-field terrain which damaged some low-slung belly tanks. "This resulted in the distortion of the tank and leakage of fuel, which provided the hazard of fire immediately upon takeoff," Parker noted. (The aft-positioned turbosupercharger hot exhaust outlet must have caused concern in this regard.) Parker also suggested that in the future, Thunderbolts should not be shipped with drop tanks attached because some of them received damage while mounted to airframes that were being unloaded from ships and routed down streets to the airfield.[18]

Flying in a combat aircraft is often exhilarating, but seldom comfortable. Republic pilot Joseph Parker said the batch of P-47Ds he accompanied to North Africa "still have smoke in the cockpit in normal power climbs." While preparing these Thunderbolts for combat, Parker's crew cut away part of the lower cowl flaps to promote cooler engine temperatures below 20,000 feet. They also installed a propeller spinner on one of the P-47s, he recounted. The spinner "… seemed to reduce the cylinder head temperatures in proportion to the cowl flap cut away. At extra high altitude, the temperatures were the same as the airplane without the spinner and without cowl flaps cut," Parker reported.[19]

Parker's crew experimented with wet-sanding the finish of the P-47s with 00-grit sandpaper to make it smoother than when the P-47s arrived. He claimed a gain in airspeed of up to 12 miles an hour from the sanding and from refitting some of the fillets; whether or not this much of a speed boost was quantifiable, the lesson was clear: Fit and finish counted when speed was important.[20]

The receiving 325th Fighter Group, moving from 12th into 15th Air Force, operated Thunderbolts from November 1943 to the end of April 1944, then switching to P-51 Mustangs.

The Needs of the Eighth Air Force

When the first P-47Cs roared into combat out of England in April 1943, Eighth Air Force leaders were still looking for the ultimate escort fighter to protect their investment in daylight precision heavy bombardment. The Thunderbolt, the P-38 Lightning, and the P-51 Mustang all underwent evolutions which gave them longer legs for escorting Fortresses and Liberators deeper into continental Europe. Perceived problems with the P-38's engines contributed to the decision to seek a different ultimate expression of the escort fighter. The P-51 Mustang, once it was fitted with an additional fuselage tank as well as two underwing drop tanks, handily escorted the bombers all the way to Berlin by 1944. Eighth Air Force made its choice: The Mustang would be emphasized, and P-47s and P-38s would be shifted to other numbered air forces. Of the ten P-47-equipped

Leaking oil painted the fuselage and windscreen of P-47D 42-75163 of the 61st Fighter Squadron; the pilot safely returned to base. (U.S. Air Force)

fighter groups assigned to Eighth Air Force by the end of 1943, only one, the 56th Fighter Group, remained at the end of the war. Other former Eighth Air Force Thunderbolts were shifted to Ninth Air Force. By the month of the Normandy invasion in June 1944, 17 Thunderbolt groups were counted in England; at least 13 of these were in Ninth Air Force by that time.[21]

The storied 56th Fighter Group of Eighth Air Force tallied a record unmatched in Eighth Air Force: nearly 700 enemy aircraft destroyed in the air and another 300-plus demolished on the ground. From that unit's high scorers came the top AAF ace in Europe, Francis Gabreski, who downed 28 fighters in front of his Thunderbolt.

Aces High

The two leading high-scoring American aces of the European Theater were both Thunderbolt pilots. Colonel Francis S. Gabreski, who got into action over Pearl Harbor on 7 December 1941 in a P-40, scored his first aerial victory, against a Luftwaffe FW-190, while flying a 61st Fighter Squadron P-47D on 24 August 1943 near Dreux, France. His fourth and fifth victories, earning ace status, came together on 26 November 1943 when Gabreski downed a pair of twin-engine Me-110s southeast of Oldenburg, Germany.

Francis Gabreski mostly encountered Bf-109s and FW-190s, although his list of victories includes several twin engine Me-110s and a pair of Me-410s. The last German fighter to fall before the guns of Gabreski's Thunderbolt was a Bf-109 near Evereux, France, on 5 July 1944. Fifteen days later, while on a strafing run, Gabreski made a forced-landing in Germany and spent the remainder of the war in a POW camp.

Robert S. Johnson also spent time in the 61st and later 62nd Fighter Squadrons of the 56th Fighter Group alongside Francis Gabreski. The first of his victories came on 13 June 1943 when he was still assigned a P-47C. He ran his impressive string of victories up to 27 by the eighth day of May 1944, after which Johnson was rotated home to the United States.

[1] Letter, Capt. Joseph H. Taggart, European Theatre Officer, AC/AS, Intelligence, to Henry C. Merritt, Republic Aviation Corp., 26 August 1943. [2] *Ibid.* [3] Kit C. Carter and Robert Mueller, Compilers, *Combat Chronology, 1941-1945, U.S. Army Air Forces in World War II*, Center for Air Force History, Washington, DC, 1991. [4] *Ibid.* [5] "Tactical Employment Trials on the Republic Airplane P-47C," Report of the Army Air Forces Board, AAFSAT, Orlando, Florida, 16 February 1943. [6] *Ibid.* [7] *Ibid.* [8] *Ibid.* [9] *Ibid.* [10] *Ibid.* [11] *Ibid.* [12] *Ibid.* [13] *Ibid.* [14] *Ibid.* [15] *Ibid.* [16] "Report on Operation of P-47 Airplanes in North Africa as Described by Mr. J.F.B. Parker, Republic's Chief Test Pilot," Republic Aviation Corporation, Farmingdale, Long Island, New York, 16 November 1943. [17] *Ibid.* [18] *Ibid.* [19] *Ibid.* [20] *Ibid.* [21] Ray Wagner, *American Combat Planes*, Third Edition, Doubleday, Garden City, New York, 1982.

Col. Benjamin O. Davis of the 332nd Fighter Group paused in the MTO with one of the Group's razorback D-models (possibly 42-25280). Colonel Davis' headgear is a composite of British headphones and American AN-6530 goggles. (AAF)

On 22 April 1944, 56th Fighter Group P-47D 42-8426 suffered major damage, but retained enough structural integrity to protect its pilot as it came to rest in an English hedge. The requirement to document mishaps and battle damage may have skewed the surviving body of Thunderbolt photographs with a large contingent of damage illustrations. (AFHRA)

Pengie, a razorback P-47D with a penguin logo on the cowling, used bold invasion stripes and huge underwing stars. Such markings were intended to ward off mistaken Allied groundfire. (SDAM)

Its tail stripe painted lower than most, P-47D 42-74620 was photographed 1 December 1943 amid ammunition crates. By the time of the photo, edge of national insignia probably was blue painted over short-lived red surround. (AAF)

Old Man Mose of the 56th Fighter Group's 62nd Fighter Squadron was flown by Lieutenant Knafelz when photographed 29 January 1944 with a paper 108-gallon drop tank shackled to the centerline. (U.S. Air Force)

When photographed (above) with a mechanic on 8 October 1943, 56th Fighter Group P-47C 41-6211 still carried a red border surrounding the national insignia. By 25 November 1943, the same C-model was photographed (below) with evidence of dark blue or black used to repaint the edge of the insignia, replacing the red. (AAF)

In February 1945, 36th Fighter Group pilot Capt. Lane Ruehlen and a Washington Times *war correspondent identified as Mr. Flaherty crowded into a modified razorback Thunderbolt "for a flight over the front lines," according to an AAF photo caption. (AFHRA)*

P-47D 42-76430 was photographed 12 June 1944, victim of complete consumption by fire. (AFHRA)

Pistol Packin' Mama of the 56th Fighter Group came to rest in England with a collapsed tailwheel 14 January 1944, with a large jagged battle-damage hole ripped in the fuselage above the letter "V". (AAF)

Spider-webbed safety glass windscreen attested to an impact this ETO Thunderbolt received on a mission. A circular rearview mirror was used on this example instead of the lower hooded housing. (AFHRA)

A P-47C (41-6330) took this hit to its windscreen during a mission over Europe in August 1943. (AAF)

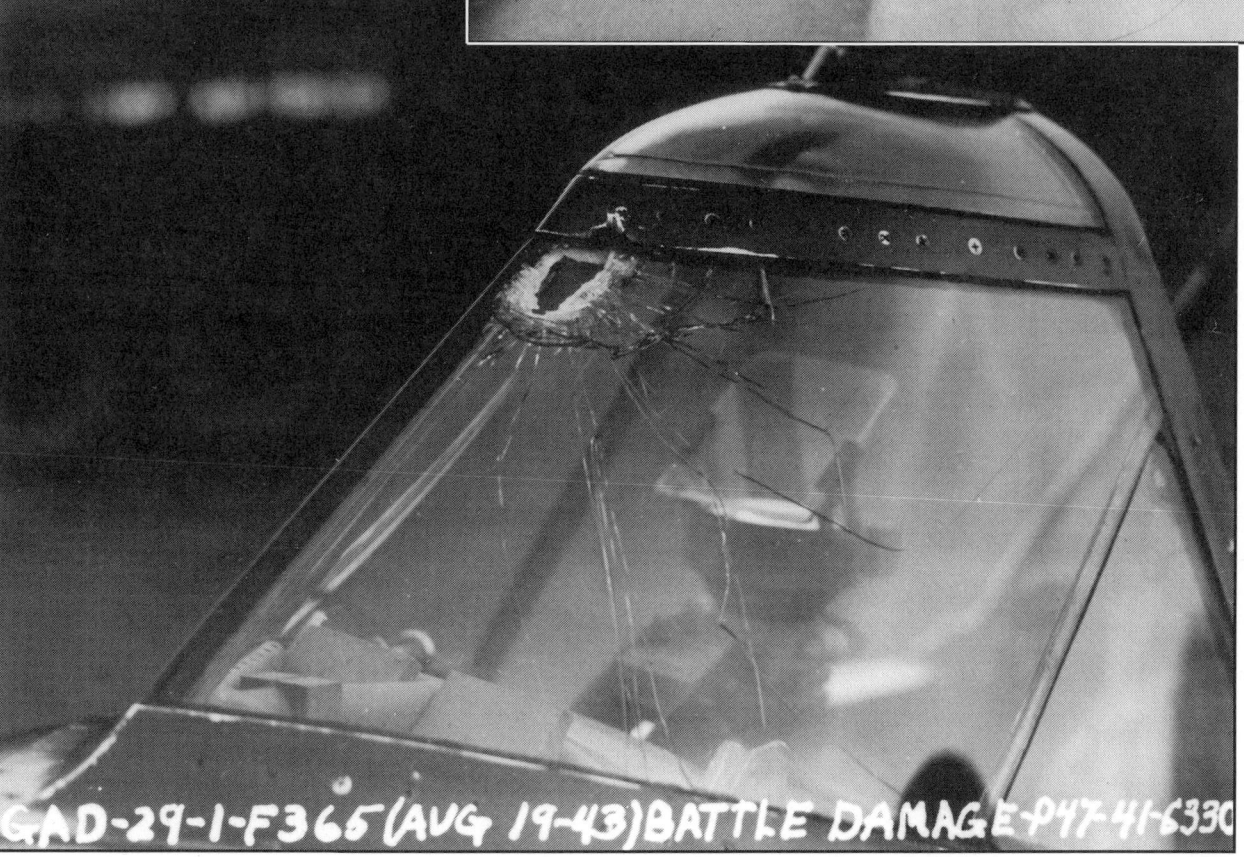

Customized markings at first glance make this appear to be a 10-gun P-47; outboard circle was painted on wing leading edge. This ETO P-47 took a hit above one of the real gun muzzles. (AFHRA)

P-47C (41-6608) represented first combat-worthy Thunderbolt variant. Guns have been removed from this noncombatant example. (U.S. Air Force via SDAM)

This Curtiss P-47G-1 (42-24965) shows Curtiss' variation in application of the tail numbers. Opened cowl flaps encircle upper hemisphere of the cowling. (Peter M. Bowers Collection)

THE COLOR OF THUNDER

P-47 Paint and Markings

P-47 Thunderbolts left the factory in olive drab and gray, and later, natural metal finish. In Europe, variations of tiger stripe camouflage and use of star insignia on both wings stood out.

Some Pacific P-47s also used bold colors to identify them to friendly forces. The 342nd Fighter Squadron of Fifth Air Force explained in January 1945: "Coloring our planes has aided greatly in helping other friendly aircraft to identify us as friendly. Planes have been painted with red, white, and blue stripes on the tail and black and white stripes on both wings and on the fuselage behind the canopy."[1]

In May 1944, a report relayed from a P-47 unit assigned to the Southwest Pacific Area (SWPA) described a determined air-to-air melee with Japanese fighters who sprung a trap over Wewak. Most Allied fighters in the SWPA had adopted white tail markings and wing leading edges as quick identification features to rapidly distinguish them from Japanese aircraft. As the Thunderbolts over Wewak dived on a pair of brightly visible silver Japanese fighters at 1,000 feet, other Japanese fighters descended behind the P-47s. In the ensuing fight, the Thunderbolt pilots observed, "on several occasions the enemy fighters passed up planes which had no white tails or white markings. Two enemy were seen with wings similar to a P-47. The enemy may have mistaken our unmarked P-47s for friendly Tojos [Nakajima Ki-44 fighters]."[2]

[1] Letter, HQ VFC, Subj: "Combat Evaluation Report," 22 January 1945. [2] "Tactical Notes — Thunderbolt (P-47)," by Lt. Col. George B. Dent, Jr., Acting Chief, Intelligence Section, Office of AC/AS, OPT&I, Headquarters, Eastern Air Command, 21 July 1944.

The Belle of Belmont, *an invasion-striped veteran 56th Fighter Group P-47D, taxied toward the Boxted runway. (Brown/USAFA)*

Natural metal finish 56th Fighter Group P-47D shows typical olive drab anti-glare panel extending behind bubble canopy, but not covering framing of canopy or windscreen. (Brown/USAFA)

When invasion stripes were removed from the tops of fuselages in about July 1944, this 56th Fighter Group razorback appears to have had the task accomplished simply by overpainting the fuselage. To preserve visibility of white call letter "N" where it impinges white invasion stripe, the color was reversed to black on the letter. (Brown/USAFA)

Sheen is visible on green and gray camouflage applied to Lt. Col. David C. Schilling's 56th Fighter Group P-47D preparing for takeoff from Boxted. Fourteen victory crosses are evident beside cockpit. (Brown/USAFA)

A spoof of the movie *I Wanted Wings* featured a disgruntled Donald Duck behind German bars in a POW camp, as depicted on the nose of a 56th Fighter Group razorback P-47D. (Brown/USAFA)

An armorer cleans a smooth-jacketed M-2 .50-caliber machine gun evidently removed from the left wing of the pin-up adorned Thunderbolt behind him, at the 56th Fighter Group area at Boxted. (Brown/USAFA)

Mixed markings and models of 56th Fighter Group Thunderbolts go to war in a roaring queue at the end of the Boxted runway. (Brown/USAFA)

REPUBLIC P-47 THUNDERBOLT

Brightly painted life raft-dropping P-47Ds of the 65th Fighter Wing Detachment B, commonly called simply the Air Sea Rescue Squadron, carried prominent invasion stripes for low-level work. Overspray frequently caused white ghosts around the invasion stripes. The unit logged 3481 Thunderbolt sorties beginning in May 1944 from Boxted. Later, OA-10As and SB-17s were used also when the unit moved to Halesworth. "WW" on tail indicated "war-weary" status of aircraft no longer considered first-line. (Brown/USAFA)

"Red-E-Ruth," a P-47N from the 318th Fighter Group, merged blue cowl flaps with black anti-glare panel on Ie Shima in 1945. (Jim Weir via Tom Foote)

At the giant Experimental Aircraft Association event in Oshkosh, Wisconsin, in 1995, Connie Bowlin waited her turn for take-off in a P-47D representing a 406th Fighter Group example as seen on the Continent. (Frederick A. Johnsen)

Thunderbolt Action
1944-1945

On the second day of 1944, Thunderbolts of the only P-47 group then remaining in 15th Air Force flew an uneventful sweep over Rome. They repeated this the following day, after providing top cover escort for B-17s during a portion of the bombers' mission. On the 12th of January, the P-47s of 15th Air Force did more than merely sweep Rome; they dropped down to strafe marshaling yards at Teramo and structures between the Tesino and Tronto Rivers. On the 20th of the month, 15th AF Jugs escorted transport aircraft on a mission to Yugoslavia. (C-47s based in Italy sometimes flew supply drops to partisans in German-held Yugoslavia, and on a few occasions the transports even landed in remote areas to pick up downed American fliers.) During this period, Thunderbolts also flew combat for Pacific air forces including Fifth and 13th AFs. Twelfth Air Force P-47s dropped bombs on Axis supply dumps near Valmontone, Italy on 17 February 1944, the same day that 16 of their Fifth Air Force counterparts strafed Japanese targets of opportunity in the vicinity of Alexishafen.[1]

The first day of March 1944 saw 12th Air Force P-47s attack a 2000-ton ship they caught in the Adriatic Sea. Next day, Thunderbolts of Fifth Air Force, giving top cover to more than 60 A-20s and B-25s over Los Negros, claimed shooting down seven Japanese fighters. On 15 March 1944, a pair of Eighth Air Force P-47s, each lugging two 1,000-pound bombs, and escorted by a half-dozen other Thunderbolts, attacked a German barge in the Zuider Zee as a feasibility test of this type of mission. Near misses were observed.[2]

P-47s sometimes made morning calls on German fighter airfields in France in an effort to disrupt the Luftwaffe before Eighth Air Force heavy bombers flew overhead to their targets. In the Mediterranean

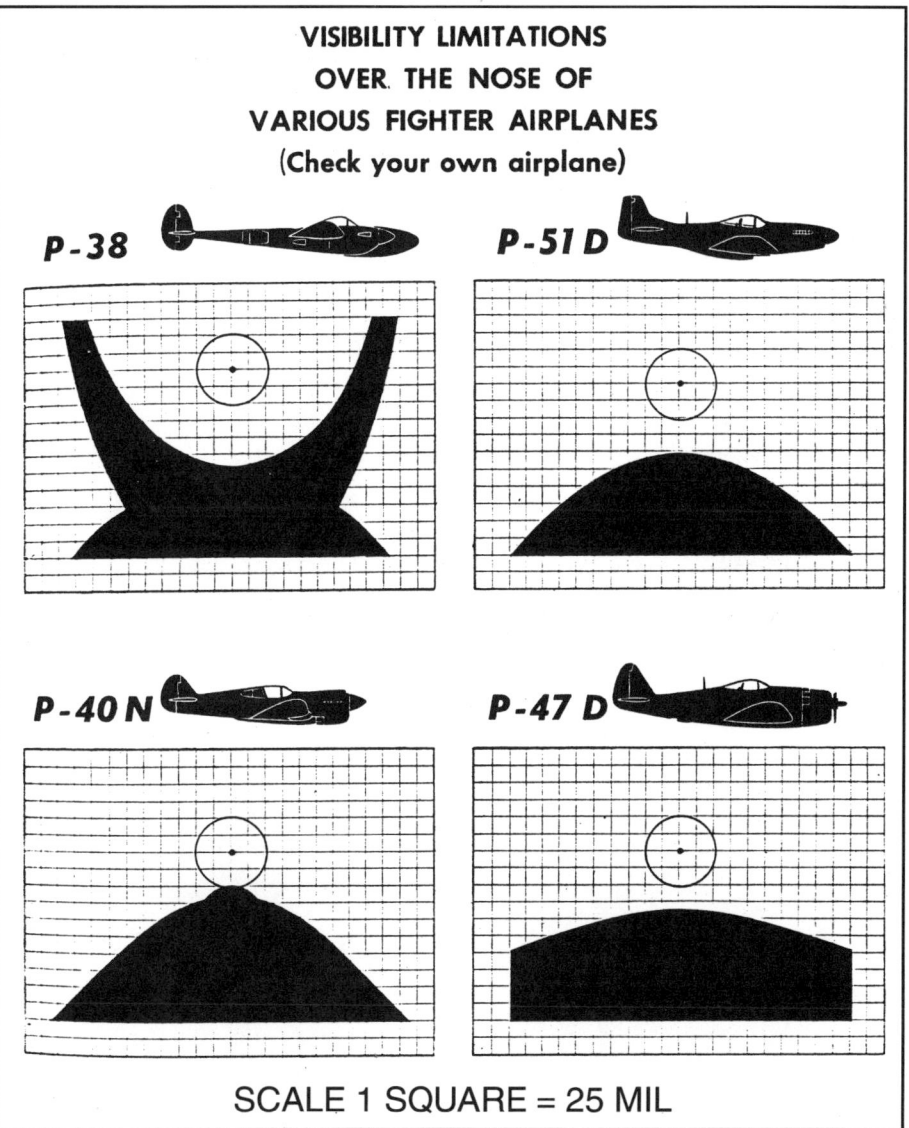

Drawings depict visibility over the noses of predominant World War Two AAF fighters. In tight turns, the need to lead an aerial adversary meant the targeted aircraft might be eclipsed from sight by the nose of the attacking fighter. (Drawing from Air Forces Manual No. 64 – Fighter Gunnery, Rocket Firing, Dive Bombing, 1 May 1945.)

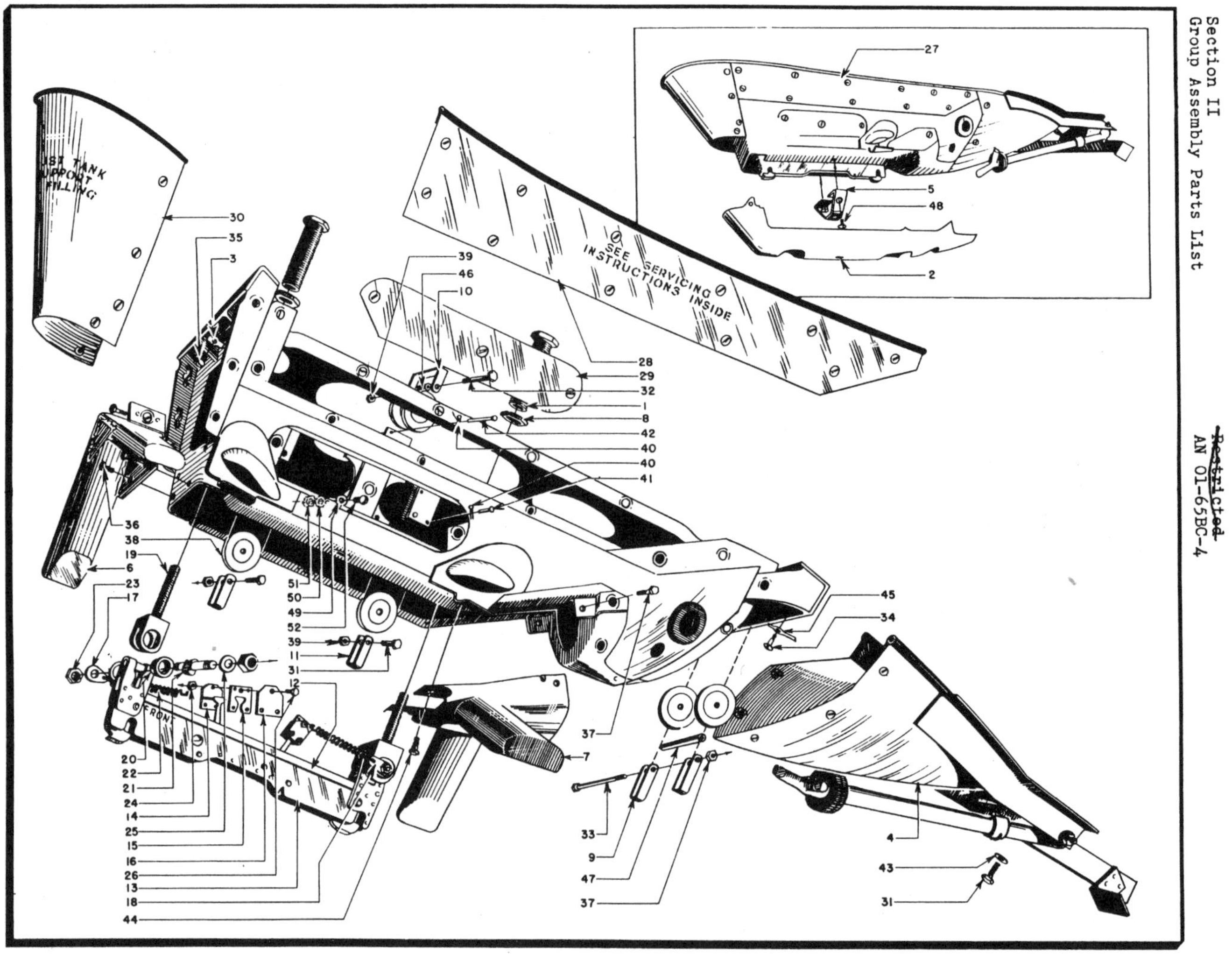

Figure 192 – Adapter Installation Wing Tank

P-47 wing pylon fairing with B-10 bomb shackle for ordnance or gasoline tank is shown in exploded view from a Thunderbolt illustrated parts book. (AAF)

Wood planks were used to adapt captured German gasoline tanks to the shackles and sway braces of the P-47. (AAF)

The banded gasoline tank in the photo would be far more at home on a Bf-109 than on a Ninth Air Force Thunderbolt wing pylon. Mechanics of the 10th Air Depot Group showed it was possible to plumb captured German drop tanks and hang them from P-47s as the Allies moved eastward on the continent in late 1944. (AAF)

Clamps, hoses, and bent aluminum tubing facilitated the mating of captured German 285-liter drop tanks to a P-47 centerline shackle. (AAF)

Theater in the spring of 1944, Thunderbolts attacked targets in Rome and at the hotly-contested Anzio beach head. On 13 April, four dozen Ninth Air Force P-47s dive-bombed German V-weapon sites on the Continent. As 1944 progressed, Thunderbolts over Italy contributed bombs and the withering fire of their machine guns to Operation Strangle, a concerted effort from March into May to cut off German forces from their supply lines to the north.

Still experimenting with bomb delivery techniques, Eighth Air Force sent a force of 79 Thunderbolts against Gutersloh airfield on 31 May 1944. Some of the P-47s dive-bombed while other Thunderbolts followed the lead of a Droopsnoot P-38 equipped with a bombsight and bombardier in a Plexiglas nose. During the days following the 6 June Normandy invasion, P-47s attacked communications targets in France; on 12 June, a group of Thunderbolts was challenged by about 50 German fighters in a determined air battle that resulted in the uneven trade of eight downed P-47s for five Messerschmitt Bf-109s. And in the Pacific, by the last week of June 1944, Seventh Air Force P-47s on Saipan were flying repeated reconnais-

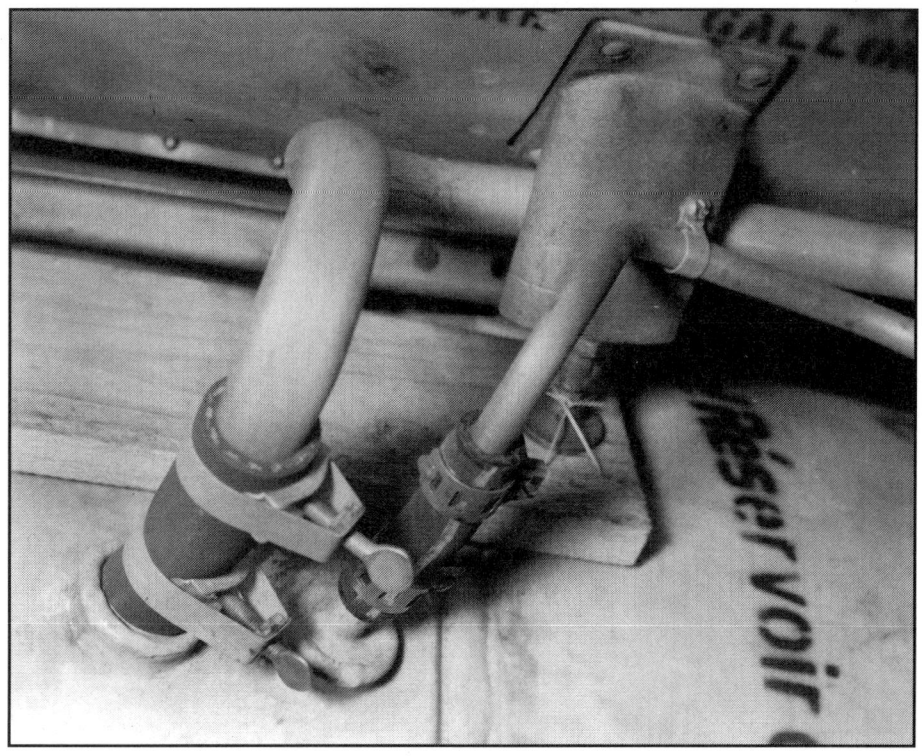

sance sorties, attacking Japanese forces remaining on Saipan as well as on Tinian and Rota.[3]

By the Fourth of July, 10th Air Force was including P-47s in its roster of fighter-bombers flying an offensive sweep over Lashio. Throughout the month, the AAF kept pressure on Axis targets in several combat theaters with Thunderbolts employed for interdiction sorties and bomber escort duties. In August, 12th Air Force P-47s turned their firepower against targets in southern France in support of the Allied landings there, as the Axis turf grew ever smaller. Thirty-two P-47 sorties by 10th Air Force supported British advances along a railroad in the vicinity of Pinbaw on 23 August 1944. River boats became fair game for 10th AF Thunderbolts in the area near Bhamo on the first day of September. That day, no fewer than seven P-47 groups bombed and strafed tracks in France and an airfield west of Nancy, during which the Thunderbolts made claims for five Luftwaffe aircraft downed in flight and five more destroyed on the ground. Starting on 11 September, Seventh Air Force P-47s from Saipan launched rockets and bombs against Japanese targets on Pagan, visiting daily for nearly a week. This target would continue to draw the interest of P-47s well into December 1944.[4]

Three-wheeled dolly with adjustable cradles was used to position a bomb by the right wing pylon of a 318th Fighter Group Thunderbolt in the Pacific. With the weight of the aircraft on the landing gear, the main gear doors overlapped each other. (Tom Foote Collection)

Even after the introduction of long-ranging P-51Bs, Cs, and Ds, P-47s still found opportunity to escort the heavy bombers over Europe as on 11 October 1944, when three Thunderbolt groups supported 130 B-17s in their effort to bomb the Wesseling synthetic oil plant and the marshaling yards at Koblenz. Nonetheless, mathematics tipped the balance in favor of ground attack for many American fighters as production capacity

Making the potent even more so, this P-47N carried 10 five-inch high velocity aircraft rockets (HVARs), as well as lugging a pair of 1,000-pound general-purpose bombs. (Peter M. Bowers Collection)

in the United States was robust, even as Axis forces were losing operational fighters at an increasing rate. In late 1944 and into 1945, Thunderbolts of 10th Air Force often supported ground troops around the Irriwaddy River. On 27 January 1945, 57th Fighter Group P-47s demolished an oil plant near Forno di Taro as part of 12th Air Force's unceasing pressure on German forces in Italy. On 12 March 1945, 12th Air Force Thunderbolts ranged up over Zagreb to bomb a munitions factory northwest of the city, inflicting measurable damage. When 12th AF P-47s ranged over the Po River area on 2 April, they were challenged by a force of about 40 German fighters, 13 of which the Thunderbolt pilots claimed as victories.[5]

The reach of the Thunderbolt included sweeps of Truk by 20 Seventh Air Force P-47s from Saipan on 28, 29, and 30 April 1945, during which the fighters strafed small ships as well as the airfields at Moen and Param, sometimes using rockets as well. On 7 May 1945, the day the German High Command made its unconditional surrender effective two days hence, 12th Air Force P-47s were aloft on a reconnaissance of the Austrian Alps. As the 318th Fighter Group was in the process of moving up to Ie Shima, on 17 May 1945 a pair of that unit's P-47s flew a heckling mission over Kyushu, the first time Seventh Air Force had mounted such a mission against Japan. When three dozen P-47s from Ie Shima swept over the southern part of Kyushu on 6 June, seeking targets of opportunity, they claimed nine Japanese aircraft shot down in addition to their air-to-ground attacks. During the summer of 1945, 14th Air Force Thunderbolts were part of the mix of fighter-bombers challenging the Japanese withdrawal from China. P-47s also escorted B-29s over Japan, as on 7 August when Far East Air Forces (FEAF) Thunderbolts shepherded a Superfortress strike at targets on Kyushu. The next day, Thunderbolts escorting B-29s claimed 10 Japanese aircraft downed. Then, on 14 August, FEAF P-47s over the Osaka-Nagoya vicinity claimed several Japanese fighters shot down in what may have been the final air-to-air victories for American-manned Thunderbolts.[6]

If, in hindsight, the outcome of World War Two appears to be an inevitable Allied victory, that fate did not come easy. The Thunderbolt and its pilots and ground crews contributed mightily to victory, facing death in the skies for more than two years running.

In the summer of 1944, Ninth Air Force razorback P-47Ds took up residence in France at a field shared by cows and a Royal Air Force Spitfire on its belly. Wraparound invasion stripes suggest this photo was taken before the end of July. (AAF)

Thanks for the Tanks

As the Allies moved through Europe following the Normandy invasion of 6 June 1944, air bases were established on the Continent, placing fighters closer to their foe. When maintenance men of the 10th Air Depot Group came across quantities of abandoned German 285-liter drop tanks, the Luftwaffe's loss stood to be the AAF's gain. By November 1944, the depot had jury-rigged three German drop tanks (part number 8-4159C-1, according to 10th Air Depot records) to a P-47.[7]

The conversion to Thunderbolt use required local fabrication of appropriate fuel and pressure lines from one-half-inch and one-inch aluminum tubing. Wooden pads and braces helped fit the German tanks to the American fighters. The AAF maintenance document describing the procedure does not indicate whether this enterprising venture saw widespread use or not.

A couple of Ninth Air Force P-47 pilots interviewed by the AAF upon their return from combat in 1945 said they had dropped German-made fire bomb casings filled with American jellied gasoline as fire bombs, indicating another use of captured Axis stores by adaptable P-47 outfits.[8]

Stretching Range in the Pacific

Fifth Fighter Command's 40th Fighter Squadron shared tips on increasing P-47D range in the last half of 1944: "The longest range mission we have flown is 835 miles… Our gas load on each mission was 775 gallons, 270 gallon main tank, 100 gallon auxiliary tank, two external wing tanks of 165 gallon capacity each, and a 75-gallon belly tank… For take-off with this gas load our policy is to use about one-third flaps, close canopy, close cowl flaps to one-third open, and use water injection to 64 inches mercury (64"HG). With a dead calm the length of the run should be no more than 4,500 feet. The safe airspeed for take-off being a minimum of 130 M.P.H. The tail should be raised as soon as possible and held high until flying speed is attained… Once in the air the pilot should start considering the conservation of fuel. Mercury and R.P.M. should be cut back as soon as safe to do so and fuel selector switched to an external tank."[9]

For these long-range missions, the climb to cruise altitude was made at an indicated airspeed of 180 miles an hour with P-47s widely spaced (probably to preclude throttle-jockeying tight formations that could eat more gas.) Cruise speed to the destination was at 190 miles an hour indicated. A Fifth Fighter Command report instructed: "The pro-

One way to compensate for the blind spot produced by the huge nose of a taxiing Thunderbolt was to place a scanner on the wing, where he could look ahead, while the pilot, Maj. Glenn T. Eagleston, watched for signals from the scanner. The highly-decorated Thunderbolt of the Ninth Air Force's 354th Fighter Bomber Group taxied on pierced steel planking at a forward airfield in France, circa January 1945, as a helmeted scanner gripped the wing leading edge with his left hand while gesturing with his right. (AAF)

Armorers in England loaded 4.5-inch rockets into tube launchers beneath the wing of a P-47, circa October 1944. (AAF)

cedure recommended for selecting tanks is as follows: (a) Use of belly tank first and drop it. (b) Use wing tanks, running them out evenly (one-half hour on first, then use one hour on each alternately). (c) In order to use belly tank first, altitude for first hour should not exceed 5,000 feet, as most belly tanks do not feed well above this altitude."[10]

The carefully-managed Thunderbolts could arrive over their target with about 20 to 30 minutes of gasoline in the external wing tanks. If contact was made with the Japanese, the wing tanks would be dropped. According to the Fifth Fighter Command description: "As gas will have siphoned back into the main tank enroute to the target, there should be at least 260 gallons now in the main tank, and the 100-gallon auxiliary has not been tapped... A safe minimum with which to leave the target is 310 gallons. Thus with 260 gallons in main tank, the auxiliary can be run out to 50 gallons."[11]

Thunderbolt and Oscar

In the spring of 1944, a report from the Southwest Pacific Area (SWPA) compared characteristics of a P-47 flown against a captured Nakajima Ki-43 Hayabusa fighter, given the Allied code name Oscar. The captured Hayabusa was described in the AAF summary as a "Type 1 F Oscar Mk 1."[12] As a Ki-43-I variant, its top speed was probably around 308 miles an hour, achieved at an optimum altitude of just over 13,000 feet.[13] The Hayabusa, long overlooked in the study of Japanese warplanes because the vaunted Mitsubishi A6M Zero was accorded the status of fighter icon, deserves notice because of its maneuverability.

The captured Oscar's AAF pilot, identified in the report only as Captain Stanton, described his initial encounter with the Thunderbolt: "Met the P-47 at 3,000 feet and outclimbed it to 5,000 feet. It dove on my tail from 6,000 feet and in a steep bank to the left I easily got out of gun range in 90 degrees. In 360 degrees I was behind the P-47 but its circle was so large that it was one-and-a-half turns to the right

A variation on the P-47 tow tests involved removing the big propeller and towing the hulking Thunderbolt with a line attached to the propeller shaft. (AAF)

A deadstick P-47 glides aloft behind a towing B-17 in a stateside AAF test of the potential for snatching disabled fighters from forward fields for repairs at depots. (AAF via the National Archives)

As airfields, sometimes rustic, became available on the Continent in the summer of 1944, it was natural that some P-47s and P-51s would land there and be stranded by mechanical problems beyond local repair capabilities. One response that was tested at Muroc Army Air Base involved attaching a tow line to a P-47 with its propeller feathered, and then snatching the line with a low-flying B-17 tow aircraft. The test did not progress to actual use in Europe. (AAF via the National Archives)

before I was in effective gun range." Two truisms of the Thunderbolt were quickly verified against the Oscar: The Japanese fighter could outclimb and outturn the P-47. Captain Stanton continued: "The circle was so large that it took half a turn for the Oscar to cross it to the P-47's tail after getting behind it."[14]

The mock dogfight continued: "The Oscar looped. P-47 flying straight ahead made it easy to get on its tail," Captain Stanton said. "The Oscar then dove on the P-47 and in turns to the right and left easily stayed inside the P-47's turns."

"The P-47 pulled up into a hammerhead stall and the Oscar climbed above and gained on him, having 10 to 20 mph on the P-47 at the top of the stall. It gained 200 yards in the climb ending almost directly above the P-47." Captain Stanton described the Thunderbolt's predicament: "The P-47 was too low to loop and due to engine trouble dove for the field; the Oscar stayed with it to 300 mph then left it. I came in and landed after the P-47."[15]

In trials begun at 5,000 feet, the P-47 pilot, First Lieutenant Morrison, described one way the Oscar evaded him: "I dived 500 yards astern of the Oscar at 240 mph. The Oscar pulled up in such a vertical angle that I was unable to follow." With the Oscar perched at 6,000 feet and the Thunderbolt at

P-47D (42-28635) of the 78th Fighter Group's 83rd Fighter Squadron landed at airfield A46, Toussus LeNoble, France, in September 1944. Cowling checkers were black and white. Late use of camouflage includes undersurface gray much lighter than standard AAF gray. (Fred LePage Collection)

5,000 feet, Lieutenant Morrison chronicled: "The Oscar then dived to a position 500 yards astern of the P-47 which was indicating 210 mph. I started a 70-degree bank to the left with the Oscar turning inside me in a shooting position through a 360-degree turn. In fact, he had to weave back and forth in order not to overrun me. This maneuver was repeated to the right with the same result... The speed of the P-47 was 210 mph at the beginning and 160 mph and 150 mph at the completion." It was chilling, if safe, proof that the big P-47 was no dogfight match for the lithe Nakajima Hayabusa. The lieutenant further confirmed the perils of following a Hayabusa into a dogfight: "In the hammerhead stall the Oscar could go above the P-47 and get in a wonderful position for a straight down pass."[16]

At 10,000 feet, the agility of the Hayabusa was described by its pilot, Captain Stanton: "The P-47 dove on the Oscar from 11,000 feet and in steep turns to the right and left the Oscar was on the P-47's tail in one-and-a-half 360-degree turns in easy position for a shot." Vertical maneuvering bled airspeed down quickly in trade for altitude gained, as Captain Stanton, flying the Hayabusa, described: "The Oscar did a loop and was three-fourths finished before the P-47 started. I attempted to catch the P-47 on top of his loop but didn't have enough speed; I was right under the P-47 tail but 200 feet below. The P-47 rolled out on top of its loop and my speed had dropped to 40 mph; so when I attempted to roll out, the nose dropped and I lost 200 feet more." The Oscar wasn't the only fighter stalling out of that maneuver; up in the P-47, as Lieutenant Morrison later recounted: "I stalled out on top of my loop Immelmann. The climb was so great the Oscar could not follow."[17]

Interestingly, the pilots reported the Oscar could not follow the bulky Thunderbolt in a loop, "as the circle was too great. He [the Oscar[had plenty of room to roll out in an Immelmann [a half roll made at the top of a loop; it reverses the fighter's direction from the heading it was flying when entering the loop.[" But, after executing an Immelmann, the Oscar was out of range for a shot until the P-47 came down on the diving side of his loop, at which time the Oscar could get on the Thunderbolt's tail briefly (although in some cases the P-47's acceleration put too much distance between the two for more than a brief shot from the

The war ended for this camouflaged Ninth Air Force P-47 on 16 February 1945 in a fuel-fed blaze following a crash landing in Belgium. (Ninth Air Force photo by Sgt. Buscaino)

A 318th Fighter Group P-47N in trouble is evidence that it is possible to flip the huge Thunderbolt on its back. (Tom Foote Collection)

Hayabusa). Taking the mock battle up to 20,000 feet, the relative maneuverabilities still favored the Japanese fighter. Another telling note showed the relative strengths and weaknesses of the two adversaries: "The Oscar dove on the P-47 but couldn't catch it till it started to turn. In turns to the right and left the Oscar stayed behind and inside the P-47 in easy gun shot... Above 300 mph the P-47 left the Oscar, but in turns at any speed the Oscar stayed with the P-47."[18]

During one maneuver at 20,000 feet, Captain Stanton stalled the Hayabusa as its speed bled down to 90 miles an hour in a turn. As a reference point, the AAF captain said the stalling Oscar, "...felt just like a P-40 in a high speed stall; the nose dropped and it made [a] quarter roll and came out easily with forward stick and top rudder."

The two AAF fliers' forays with a Hayabusa and a Thunderbolt led to the conclusion in their report: "The P-47 had only one chance with the Oscar and that is: Dive away, never let your speed drop below 200 mph and do not try to stay and fight with him. If you do pull up in a loop, have plenty of speed and roll out in an Immelmann." By terminating in a half loop with an Immelmann, the fliers found they could keep the Oscar at a distance; if the P-47 finished the loop, the Oscar could at least get in one shot early in the dive phase. The pilots noted a performance fall-off in the Hayabusa beginning at 15,000 feet: "From 15,000 feet up you can climb away from the Oscar in a shallow climb with the throttle and rpm wide open."[19]

It was an interesting match between a nimble Japanese fighter with a loaded weight somewhere around two-and-a-half tons, facing an American P-47 weighing in at probably five or six tons (although the actual weights during the mock combats were not given in the report). The Hayabusa's nominal 1,150 horsepower radial engine was bested in some engagements by the Thunderbolt's 2,000 horsepower; speed was the P-47's edge.

P-47 Hampered by Hamp's Maneuverability

Another 1944 evaluation of a P-47 against a captured Japanese "Hamp" single-engine fighter (Mitsubishi A6M3 Type 0; later codenamed Zeke) produced many of the same results as the tests with the Oscar. The Hamp study contained succinct advice, in the gritty vernacular of the era: "Do not dogfight with the Jap!!! In the majority of cases it was found that the safest and most effective method of attack was to keep the air speed well up, make a pass and dive straight away."[20]

Section II
Group Assembly Parts List

Restricted
AN 01-65BC-4

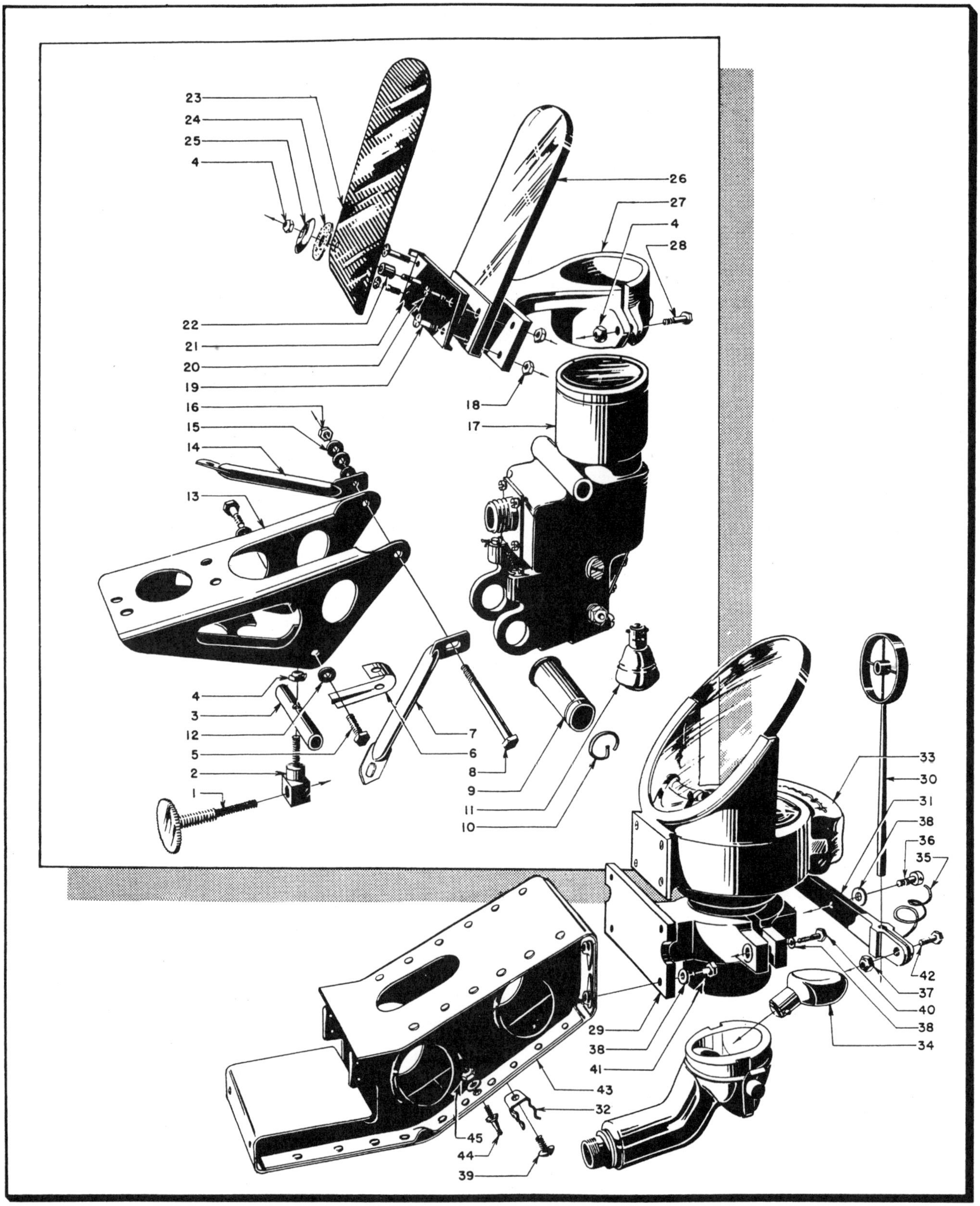

Two types of Thunderbolt gunsight and sight mount were depicted in a P-47 parts manual. Upper drawing represents N3B sight; lower artwork shows Mark VIII sight, plus back-up ring sight. (AAF)

P-47D Versus Zeke 52

The Army Air Forces compared the P-47D, a P-51D, and a P-38J in flight trials against a captured Mitsubishi A6M5 Zeke 52 fighter, with results published by the Division of Naval Intelligence in April 1945. The results of mock combats were summarized: "Due to advantages in speed, acceleration and high speed climb, all three AAF fighters were able to maintain the offensive in individual combat with the Zeke 52, and to break off combat at will. The Zeke 52 is greatly superior to all three AAF fighters in radius of turn and general maneuverability at low speeds."[21]

At 10,000 feet, the tested P-47D-30 showed a true airspeed about 70 miles an hour faster than that capable of being produced by the Zeke 52 example. At 25,000 feet, this speed differential favored the P-47 by about 90 miles an hour. During mock dogfights, several combat-seasoned Thunderbolt pilots flew against the Zeke 52, which was always flown by the same pilot. In a level turning circle, the Zeke demonstrated its ability to outturn the P-47D in one-half to three-fourths of a turn. Aileron rolls showed the Zeke to be faster-rolling than the Thunderbolt in speeds between 180 and 250 miles an hour indicated airspeed; around 250 miles an hour, the roll rates for the two combatants were about equal; above that speed, according to the evaluation report, "the P-47D's rate of roll became increasingly superior to the Zeke." Even though the Thunderbolt always bested the Zeke in climbing and

P-47Ms and N-models could be fitted with the sophisticated K14 gunsight. (AAF)

diving contests, adding a spiral to the equation gave the nimble Mitsubishi an exploitable edge: "In climbing and diving spirals at 10,000 and 25,000 feet, the Zeke could easily stay in range inside the turn, if starting the spiral 100 to 200 yards astern the P-47D. With the P-47D following in the spiral, the Zeke could avoid fire by out turning the P-47D after 180 degrees of either a climbing or diving spiral."[22]

Best bets for the P-47D involved fast, straight, diving passes, either to shoot at the Zeke, or to escape its gunfire, with climbing turns to put the P-47 back in position to fight made out of the Zeke's range. Turning in the vicinity of the Zeke invited disaster.[23]

Pacific P-47 Combat Intelligence

Intelligence officers circulated combat reports in an effort to keep operational units apprised of the experiences of others operating the same aircraft. From a 1944 P-47 combat report comes this glimpse of Thunderbolts in combat against Japanese forces:

An April 1944 encounter over Wewak pitted P-47s against Japanese fighters. When initially set upon

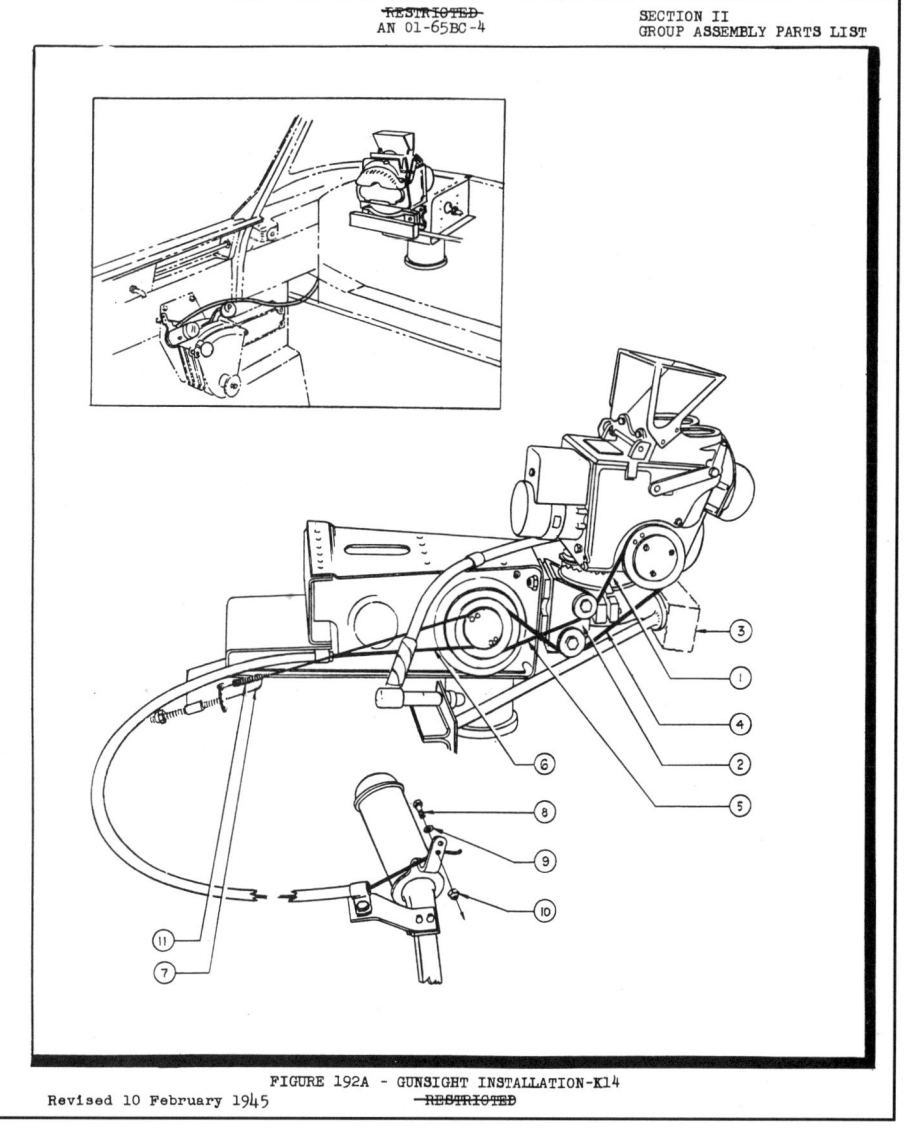

by the Japanese fighters, the Thunderbolt pilots followed "the book." and dived away to gain speed and distance between them and the enemy aircraft. The narrative of the event explained: "Having gotten away successfully the [P-47] leader and wingman zoomed back up and climbed at 20,000 feet ..." As the fight continued, "The [P-47] leader fired at a Hamp [Mitsubishi A6M3 Type 0] which escaped by a sharp turn to the right while the wingman was attacking another which got away in a dive and turn. The enemy airplanes seemed to have no trouble in turning inside the P-47." Though shots were traded, neither Japanese nor American fighters were downed in this fight.[24]

P-47 Ground Attack, ETO-Style

In April 1945, an AAF intelligence unit published information that had been gleaned from an interview with a half-dozen returning Ninth Air Force P-47 pilots regarding ground attack methods in the Thunderbolt. Their targets had included trains, bridges, troops, tanks, convoys, gun emplacements, marshaling yards, and other objects of value. The P-47 pilots painted a picture of dive-bombing technique that typically included an approach to the target at 8,000 to 12,000 feet, with some approaches flown as low as 5,000 feet, although this necessitated a shallower dive to give adequate time for sighting in the dive, they explained. The formerly-Restricted intelligence report said: "If a good steep dive is to be made, it is more important to come in right over the target with the sun at your back; either upwind or downwind. Most dives are made with planes in trail making individual runs. Diving with a wing man did not prove very satisfactory and was found to be not too accurate for the wing man since he might be in a skid when the bombs are released."[25]

The P-47 pilot interviewees agreed steeper dives contributed to bombing accuracy in Thunderbolts. "Most P-47 pilots usually went in at an angle from 60 to 70 degrees. The point of release varies with the steepness of the dive," the report noted. "In a shallow dive, the bombs should be carried as low as possible without getting into bomb blast. The pull-out was made at about 1500 to 3000 feet, usually about 3000 feet," the report said. Evasive action during the pullout was recommended, such as a low-level exit followed by a climbing turn; "a pilot should never pull straight up when trying to evade enemy flak after bombs have been released," the study noted.[26]

The six P-47 interviewees said Thunderbolt strafing attacks were usually made in line abreast formation, with a gaggle of P-47s roaring across an airfield, and not down the runway's length. "As a general rule," the report noted, "it is not advisable

Soviet P-47D was photographed with red stars encircled in white discs. Though a number of American Lend-Lease aircraft were handed over to the Soviets with this style of marking, evidence suggests the end users toned down the insignia by overpainting the bright white discs. (SDAM)

to make more than one pass at an airfield." The study continued: "Railroad trains and truck convoys should be attacked at right angles since it has been found that one or more trucks or cars are flak gun mounts which make going down the length quite dangerous." The Thunderbolt fliers sometimes began firing farther out when diving than when on low-altitude level attacks. The report added: "Sometimes they fire an experimental burst at 1000 to 2000 yards to check their guns and also to demoralize enemy troops. However, most pilots feel that the correct range to fire effectively is 300 to 600 yards." Regardless of distance, the authoritative bark of eight simultaneously-firing .50-caliber machine guns was an attention-getter. Exiting on the deck from an airfield attack was advised, unless the target was in danger of exploding and engulfing the Thunderbolt. "In all cases," the report said, "it is well to make skids and take other evasive action as soon as the strafing run is completed."[27]

The Ninth AF P-47 pilots described napalm drop tanks as having no ballistic co-efficient, meaning no predictable path for precision release. According to the report, this made it necessary for the P-47s to drop napalm "at low level anywhere from 50 to 1000 feet, either in a glide or while flying level. Since most fire bombs are supposed to cover an area of about 200 square yards, no particular accuracy is required, except to drop it right over or just ahead of the target area. The actual approach depends on the surrounding terrain and defenses. The main plan is to carry the tank right to the target because of the inability to aim it."[28]

The report stated some of the returning P-47 pilots said that after Allied troops penetrated German borders, "fire bombs were dropped on whole villages and towns and we did considerable damage." One of the Thunderbolt pilots said his group sometimes filled 100-pound practice bombs with napalm, allowing greater accuracy when placing these finned fire bombs on target. Though the interviewed P-47 pilots agreed none of them had much experience in firing rockets from their Thunderbolts, they did offer some advice for the report, including: "Two returnees agreed that it is advisable to use strafing in conjunction with firing the rockets. In this manner, a pilot can follow the trajectory of the tracers and after some practice, judge how to fire the rockets."[29]

Even though American pilots enjoyed a training environment better than their Axis contemporaries, especially as the war encroached on Germany and Japan, the interviewed veteran P-47 ground attack pilots agreed new replacement pilots lacked experience flying on instruments. The report noted: "Replacements are

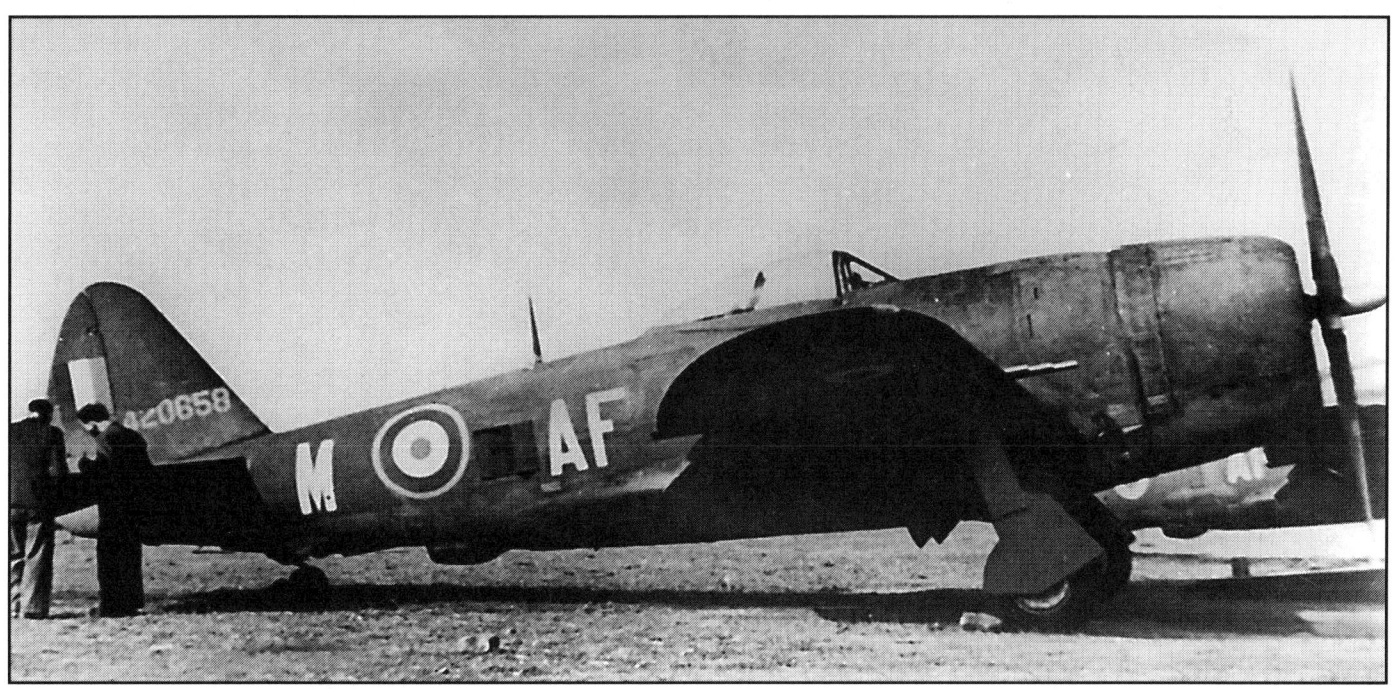

French P-47D carried tricolor flash on its rudder instead of its fixed vertical fin. French Thunderbolts served long after the war. (SDAM)

A scavenged 50th Fighter Group (10th Fighter Squadron) P-47D (42-76298) had been painted with invasion stripes that were cut out to avoid previously-applied squadron letters and numbers. (U.S. Air Force)

not allowed to fly in actual instrument weather, even for practice in the states and often their first experience flying in weather conditions might be on their first mission in a heavily loaded ship over enemy territory." The returnees said training should include more low level work, on the deck around hills and structures if possible. The report concluded: "It is the opinion of a majority of the pilots interviewed that the men new from the states have not been taught how to fight in a fighter bomber, but rather have been taught how to fly safely."[30] Granted, the sample of six P-47 pilots covered by the interview was too small to be considered universal, but it offers a vignette of the P-47 fighter-bomber pilot's war over Europe.

Mexico Goes to War In P-47s

On 5 April 1945, the 201st Mexican Fighter Squadron was attached to Fifth Fighter Command, to be effective upon the squadron's arrival in the theater. Mexican and American liaison personnel accompanied the squadron, which was attached to the 58th Fighter Group at Porac on Luzon. Under the 58th Group, the Mexican squadron had quarters, rations, supply, and operational control.[31]

On 7 and 8 May, members of the Mexican squadron were briefed at Fifth Fighter Command headquarters on the status of the ground war, weather in the southwest Pacific, fighter control and fighter sectors, escape and evasion, and air-sea rescue. During this period, the Mexican Thunderbolt pilots also underwent practical combat training for more than three weeks. Actual combat sorties began on 1 June 1945 and ran through 10 July. The Mexican fliers participated in 50 missions, amassing 293 combat sorties. The 201st Mexican Fighter Squadron averaged 17 P-47s, and had a peak strength of 32 pilots. As reported in the Fifth Fighter Command history: "Operations were almost entirely in support of ground forces on Luzon, although a few flights were made to Formosa."[32]

In the course of combat, the Mexican Thunderbolt pilots used 181 tons of bombs and expended 104,000 rounds of .50-caliber ammunition. Seven Mexican pilots were listed as killed or missing; five of these men were lost during the squadron's last 10 days of combat.[33]

Brazil was another wartime recipient of 66 P-47Ds, some of which saw service with a Brazilian squadron deployed to Italy which began operations in the fall of 1944.[34]

The Royal Air Force received about 800 various razorback and bubble-top P-47Ds, identified as Thunderbolt I and Thunderbolt II, respectively. By September 1944, RAF Thunderbolts were in service over Burma. Thunderbolts eventually equipped a dozen British squadrons by the end of the war. French allocations numbered 446 D-models; the red star of the Soviet Union adorned slightly more than 200 razorback and bubble-top P-47Ds.[35]

AAF Thunderbolts served in the Pacific, China-Burma-India, Mediterranean, and European Theaters of Operations. They escorted bombers, challenged enemy fighters, bombed Axis surface transportation, and carried rafts to drop to ditched crews. Statisticians credit P-47s with destroying better than four-and-a-half enemy aircraft for each Thunderbolt lost in air-to-air fighting. P-47s fired more than 135 million rounds of .50-caliber bullets. Slightly more than half of all overseas Thunderbolts were written off due to all causes including enemy action.

The lack of freshly disturbed snow suggests these photos of a Ninth Air Force P-47 pilot inspecting the results of his latest belly-landing may have been staged somewhat after the event. Peg O' My Heart flew with the 391st Fighter Squadron of the 366th Fighter Group. (Ninth Air Force)

[1] Kit C. Carter and Robert Mueller, Compilers, *Combat Chronology, 1941-1945, U.S. Army Air Forces in World War II*, Center for Air Force History, Washington, DC, 1991. [2] *Ibid.* [3] *Ibid.* [4] *Ibid.* [5] *Ibid.* [6] *Ibid.* [7] Report, "Draft THTI Amendment," by Capt. George J. Goodheart, Asst. Chief of Maintenance, Maintenance Division, 10th Air Depot Group, 11 Nov 44 (Filed at AFHRA). [8] Report: "Dive Bombing, Strafing, Rocket Firing and Fire Bombing," Air Intelligence Contact Unit, Headquarters AAF Redistribution Station No. 2, Miami District, AAFPDC, Miami Beach, Florida, 5 April 1945. [9] "History of V Fighter Command", Annex 1, July-December 1944. [10] *Ibid.* [11] *Ibid.* [12] "Tactical Notes — Thunderbolt (P-47)," by Lt. Col. George B. Dent, Jr., Acting Chief, Intelligence Section, Office of AC/AS, OPT&I, Headquarters, Eastern Air Command, 21 July 1944. [13] Rene J. Francillon, *Japanese Aircraft of the Pacific War*, Naval Institute Press, Annapolis, Maryland, 1988. [14] "Tactical Notes — Thunderbolt (P-47)," by Lt. Col. George B. Dent, Jr., Acting Chief, Intelligence Section, Office of AC/AS, OPT&I, Headquarters, Eastern Air Command, 21 July 1944. [15] *Ibid.* [16] *Ibid.* [17] *Ibid.* [18] *Ibid.* [19] *Ibid.* [20] *Ibid.* [21] "Comparative Performance Between Zeke 52 and the P-38, P-51, P-47," Technical Air Intelligence Center Report #38, Naval Air Station Anacostia, D.C., April 1945. [22] *Ibid.* [23] *Ibid.* [24] "Tactical Notes — Thunderbolt (P-47)," by Lt. Col. George B. Dent, Jr., Acting Chief, Intelligence Section, Office of AC/AS, OPT&I, Headquarters, Eastern Air Command, 21 July 1944. [25] Report: "Dive Bombing, Strafing, Rocket Firing and Fire Bombing," Air Intelligence Contact Unit, Headquarters AAF Redistribution Station No. 2, Miami District, AAFPDC, Miami Beach, Florida, 5 April 1945. [26] *Ibid.* [27] *Ibid.* [28] *Ibid.* [29] *Ibid.* [30] *Ibid.* [31] "History of V Fighter Command," Narrative, Chapter 6, 1 April-2 September 1945. [32] *Ibid.* [33] *Ibid.* [34] Ray Wagner, *American Combat Planes*, Third Edition, Doubleday, Garden City, New York, 1982. [35] *Ibid.* [36] William Green, *Famous Fighters of the Second World War*, Volume 1, Doubleday, Garden City, New York, 1962.

REPUBLIC **P-47 THUNDERBOLT**

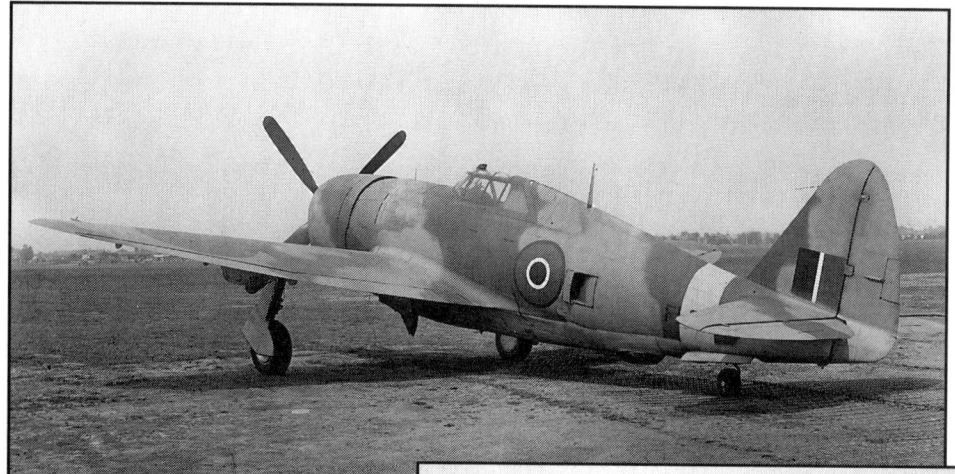

Razorback Thunderbolt I of the Royal Air Force showed RAF fuselage roundel placement forward of the turbosupercharger doors. The Thunderbolt II shown below used nominally the same camouflage scheme applied to the razorback Thunderbolt I. (Peter M. Bowers Collection)

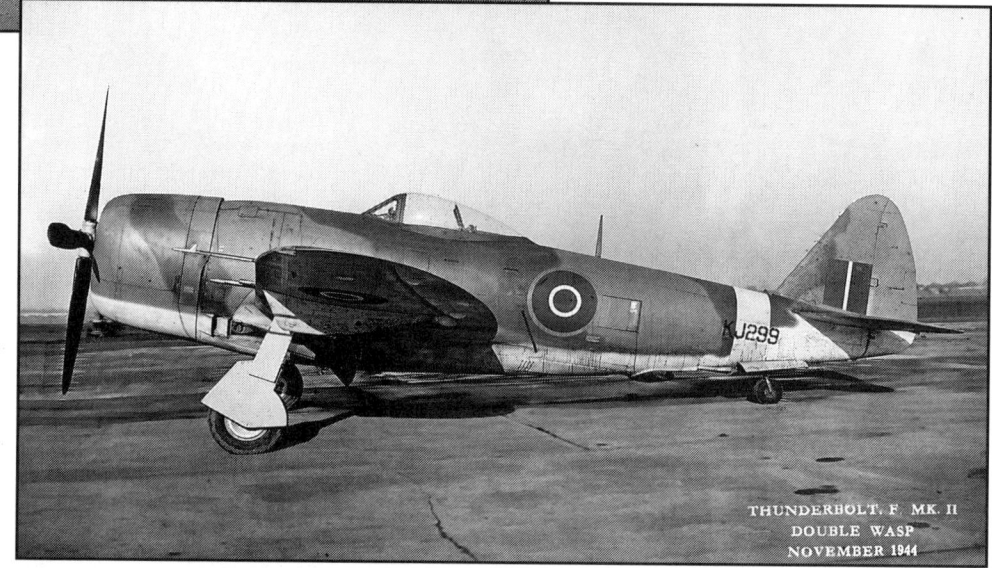

The shade variations in insignia indicate the top photo was made with orthochromatic film while the Thunderbolt II at right was photographed using panchromatic film, sensitive to all colors. When used in the CBI Theater, RAF Thunderbolts replaced the full-color insignia seen here with toned-down versions eliminating read, and sometimes replacing the bright white with pale blue. (Peter M. Bowers Collection)

The safety glass on this Eighth Air Force P-47 crystallized from a combat impact. (AFHRA)

86

P-47s After VJ-Day

Postwar Military Thunderbolts

The rapid demobilization of America's armed forces at the end of the war affected the supply system that kept the Air Force flying. In January 1947, the peacetime 23rd Fighter Group, on Northwest Field at Guam, documented the hurdles they faced in trying to keep their P-47Ns flying: "Flying training for the month of January began at a great rate. Over five hundred (500) hours were flown in the first week. On January 7 the Group received Twenty P-47Ns from GAMA which had been in storage at Harmon Field. These aircraft were turned over to the 614th Air Engineering Squadron for necessary inspections and un-pickling before being assigned to the Fighter Squadrons. Then operations ceased to be such a smooth running machine, for on January 14 all Fighter aircraft were grounded. But even this difficulty did not prevent the 23rd Group from surpassing their previously set goal of 1000 flying hours for the month of January."[1]

The plucky P-47 pilots on Guam in 1947 did the best they could: "Pilots did not complete the required night time because our P-47s are not equipped with operative flight instruments. However, the installation of these instruments is contemplated in the near future, depending of course, upon Tech Supply."[2]

Republic reunion in the sky saw a brace of Iranian Air Force P-47s escort an Iranian F-84 Thunderjet. Abundance of P-47s phased out by the U.S. Air Force made them available to foreign users. (SDAM)

The Air National Guard

Various state units of the Air National Guard received Thunderbolts in the early postwar years. Units from many states — and the territories of Hawaii and Puerto Rico — flew P/F-47s ranging from 1946 until the last Guard Thunderbolt was phased out in 1955. (For a list of Thunderbolt Air National Guard units, see Appendix 1.)

In 1967, a group of volunteers from the Puerto Rico Air National Guard began resuscitating a P-47N that had been retired to a local vocational school in San Juan, Puerto Rico, more than a decade earlier. For the next three years, their donated efforts, estimated to include 6,000 manhours, went into making the Thunderbolt airworthy. Some parts were found in the inventories of the Venezuelan and Dominican Republic air forces; other items were located on the open market.[3] The P-47N was flown for a number of years as a tribute to the Thunderbolt and the Puerto Rico Air National Guard. Later it was reported moved to the collection of the Air Force Armament Museum at Eglin Air Force Base, Florida.

Hooray for Hollywood

The survival of squadrons of Thunderbolts in the postwar Air National Guard gave Warner Brothers studios access to ample numbers of P-47s in 1948 for filming "Fighter Squadron," a fictionalized amalgamation of World War Two exploits starring Edmund O'Brien and Robert Stack, and including an earnestly eager Jack Larson, later remembered for his 1950s television portrayal of Superman's young pal, Jimmy Olson.

Eyeing the budget for the movie, a conscious choice to use Thunder-

Similarities in the air force insignia worn by members of the Ecuadorian and Colombian air forces make it difficult to positively identify this photo, but it almost certainly depicts a P-47D of one of those nations, fitted with an indigenous napalm tank, according to Central American air forces specialist Dan Hagedorn. Strut at rear of tank keeps the vessel from pivoting and striking the P-47 when released. (Lin Hendrix/SDAM)

bolts was made, to take advantage of color AAF documentary P-47 combat footage shot in Italy. Four Air National Guard Thunderbolt squadrons furnished aircraft and pilots for the filming, which took place at Oscoda airfield in Michigan. The Jugs were repainted to match the 57th Fighter Group aircraft in the borrowed combat footage. If critics found the film somewhat cliché-ridden, the public responded well to it nonetheless. A hallmark was the dramatic P-47 footage, both wartime and purpose-shot for the movie.[4]

Fire Bomber Test

Tests performed at Eglin Field, Florida, in the summer of 1947 involved releasing a pair of water-bomb 165-gallon drop tanks from a P-47N for use in firefighting. That July, a contingent of two P-47Ns, one B-29, and a B-25 used for liaison, flew up to Great Falls, Montana, to further test the theory of drenching fires with water-filled drop tanks. Following sorties against test fires in the Lolo National Forest, the Thunderbolts and the Superfortress were pitted against actual wildfires in western Montana.[5]

The P-47Ns tried finned and unfinned tank variants, dropping a total of 56 tanks in dive- and glide-bombing runs. Unlike some of the B-29 tanks, which were fused to rupture above the fire, the Thunderbolts' drop tanks relied on hitting the earth to spill their water over the fire area. Initial results favored the Thunderbolt method of delivery. Funding problems led to a week-long grounding of the firefighting P-47Ns in August for lack of fuel; an ambitious proposal to deploy 75 fighters as fire bombers for the 1948 season was not fulfilled.[6] Subsequent evolution of firefighting aircraft emphasized internal tanks from which liquid was dumped without being contained in a drop tank.

Foreign Military Operators

P-47s served a variety of countries after World War Two, ranging from traditional Central and South American users of American equipment, to countries as enigmatic as Yugoslavia. Nations flying Thunderbolts, including some World War Two allies as well as postwar operators, were: Bolivia, Brazil, Chile, Colombia, Cuba, England, France, Iran, Italy, Mexico, Nicaragua, Pakistan, Peru, the Soviet Union, Turkey, Venezuela, and Yugoslavia.

Mexico, whose air force had furnished pilots to fly P-47s in the Philippines during the last months of the war, received Thunderbolts from AAF stocks in November 1945. The delivery of these postwar Thunderbolts to Mexico was observed by the Laredo Army Airfield historian in Texas, who noted the transfer of the P-47s at Laredo on 29 November 1945: "Between the 15th and 20th of November, 30 P-47s arrived at this station from Middletown Depot, Pennsylvania, for transfer to the Mexican Air Forces on authority from the Commanding General, Air Technical Ser-

Postwar Mexican Air Force P-47D taxied past DC-4s at a 1954 air show in Mexico. (SDAM)

New Jersey Air National Guard P-47D-30-RA helped keep the Thunderbolt story alive in postwar American military aviation. Red bar in wing insignia shows photo to be at least 1947 or newer. (SDAM)

Cuban P-47Ds in a row show the occasional use of aluminum "hubcaps" on the inside of the main wheels on the closest aircraft, while the next Thunderbolt in line has its wheels exposed. At least one Cuban P-47D is reported to be displayed in Havana. (Dan Hagedorn Collection)

vice Command, Wright Field, Dayton, Ohio. Twenty-five P-47s were given to the 201st Fighter Squadron, Mexican Air Force, to compensate for twenty-five P-47s they left in the Philippine Islands. The five extra P-47s arrived at this station to insure prompt delivery of the necessary twenty-five aircraft on the 29th of November. A group of pilots from the 201st Mexican Fighter Squadron under the command of Major Rafael J. Suarez Peralta received the twenty-five P-47s and flew them to Mexico on 29 November 1945."[7] The five spare Thunderbolts were returned to Wright Field.

French P-47s flew a ground-attack war against Algerian rebels beginning in 1954; by 1959, Douglas Skyraiders were on hand to supplant the aging French Thunderbolts, but for naught, as Algeria gained its independence in 1962.

For Old Times' Sake

When officials at Republic Aviation decided to commemorate the 20th anniversary of the first flight of the Thunderbolt in 1961, finding a flyable P-47 was, ironically, more difficult than it would be decades later as the warbird movement later gained momentum. After following some profitless leads, Republic's Thunderbolt hunters learned of a razorback P-47 parked at the quiet desert airfield at Blythe, California. The Jug was owned by aircraft dealer Bob Bean, who bought it in the 1950s from the University of California, where the P-47 had been an aviation school teaching aid. Republic and Bob Bean came to terms on the Thunderbolt, which reportedly was sold to the company that had designed it, for the sum of $7,000.

Bob Bean made the old fighter (carrying U.S. civil registration N5087V) airworthy for its delivery to Long Island in time for the 20th anniversary reunion at Republic, where Thunderbolt pilots and builders gathered in approaching middle-age, to watch a P-47 roar overhead once more.

[1] History Report, 23rd Fighter Group, 1 January - 31 January 1947. [2] *Ibid.* [3] "PRANG Jug Saga," Jug Letter, P-47 Thunderbolt Pilots Association, Vol. IX, No. 2, Summer 1976. [4] Bruce W. Orriss, *When Hollywood Ruled the Skies — The Aviation Film Classics of World War II*, Aero Associates, Hawthorne, California, 1984. [5] "Forest Fire Air Attack System," William T. Larkins, *American Aviation Historical Society Journal*, Vol. 9, No. 3, Fall 1964. [6] *Ibid.* [7] History report, 2126 AAFBU and 2224 AAFBU, Laredo Army Airfield, Texas, November-December 1945.

Postwar P-47D shows later D-model embellishments including dorsal fin and underwing pylons. Armor plate to protect pilot's head from the rear was canted forward in bubble-top Thunderbolts. (USAFM)

Saltwater landing near the reef at Talofofo Bay on 12 November 1947 for a P-47N of the 23rd Fighter Group resulted in a wading salvage operation. (AFHRA)

To clear test airspace of nonessential traffic – especially private aircraft with no radios (NORDO) – a late-production P-47D (45-49329) acted as a flying billboard in the early postwar era. (U.S. Air Force via the Chilstrom/Warburton collections)

AN-01-65BC-4
SECTION II—GROUP ASSEMBLY PARTS LISTS

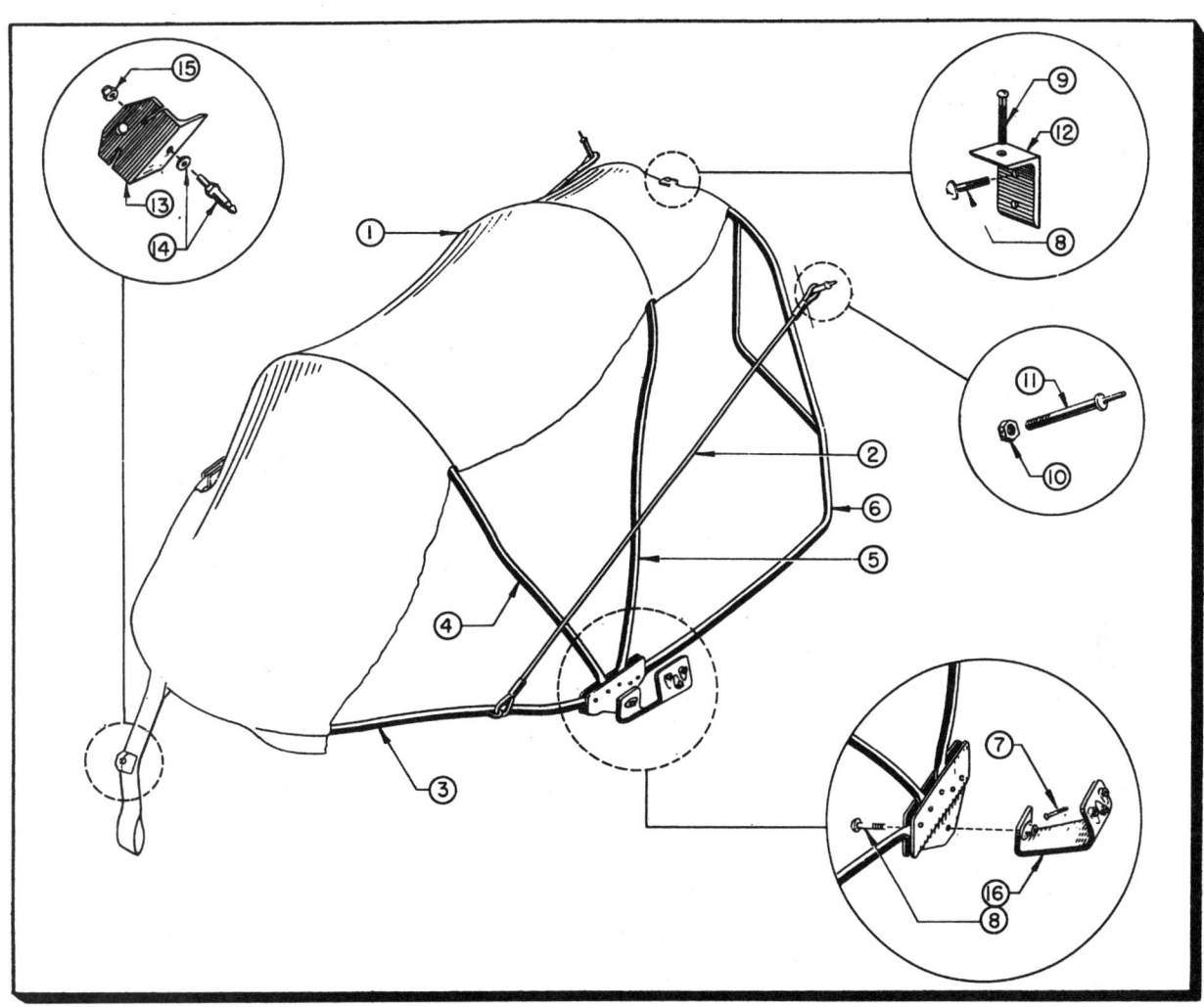

Figure 220 - Hood Installation Blind Flying

FIG. NO.	INDEX NO.	STOCKED	GROUP MAJOR ASSEMBLY PART NUMBER	EQUIPMENT 1	2	3	4	5	6	NOMENCLATURE	UNITS PER ASSY	U.S. NAVY	U.S. ARMY	BRITISH
				HOOD INSTALLATION BLIND FLYING
			*89F84110							Hood Installation Blind Flying			01-N	
220	1		89F84144							Hood Assembly	1		01-N	
220	2		89F84144-13							Cord Assembly	2		01-N	
220	3		89F84139							Bow 1 Blind Flying Hood	1		01-N	
220	4		89F84140							Bow 2 Blind Flying Hood	1		01-N	
220	5		89F84141							Bow 3 Blind Flying Hood	1		01-N	
220	6		89F84142							Bow 4 Blind Flying Hood	1		01-N	
220	7		AN505D8-10							Screw	3		29	
220	8		525D10-10							Screw	3		29	
220	9		AN515D8-12							Screw	1		29	
220	10		AN315-3R							Nut	2		04-A	
220	11		89F84150-1							Eyebolt	2		01-N	
220	12		89F84145							Clip-Tieback	1		01-N	
220	13		89F84137							Bracket-Tie Down	1		01-N	
220	14		225-9							Fastener	1		03-B	
220	15		AN365-1032							Nut	1		04-A	

A line drawing from a Thunderbolt illustrated parts book showed an extendable blind-flying hood that was designed to allow P-47 pilots an opportunity to practice flying on instruments. (AAF)

Row of P-47Ns on Guam in 1947 included aircraft of the 74th, 75th, and 76th Fighter Squadrons of the 23rd Fighter Group. It was a transitional time, as some of the Thunderbolts still had the World War Two-style insignia without red bars. Some of the P-47s were fitted with teardrop ADF antenna housings behind the cockpit. (U.S. Air Force)

The engineless airframe of the XP-47N (built without the dorsal fin extension characteristic of production N-models) served as a ground testbed for ejection seats at Wright Field, circa 1946-47, when photographed during a public demonstration. (U.S. Air Force via Chilstrom/Warburton collections)

CROWD PLEASERS

CIVILIAN AND MUSEUM P-47s

The P-47 in postwar years has always been more scarce than the P-51. If its formidable size weren't enough to draw a crowd, its novelty would be. One of the earliest newsmaking-acquisitions of warbirds from abroad was the remarkable return of six P-47s from the Peruvian air force in 1969. Refurbished by the Confederate Air Force, then headquartered at Harlingen, Texas, the half-dozen Peruvian bubble-tops soon acquired a variety of military paint schemes, and posed for group formation photos that telegraphed the burgeoning interest in warbirds. Some of the lot were subsequently sold to other warbird operators, spreading the wealth of Thunderbolts around the country, and in some cases, eventually to England.

The six Peruvian P-47Ds returned under the auspices of the Confederate Air Force (and, evidently, a New York company called Vintage Aircraft International) were (with their ex-Peruvian Air Force number in parentheses):[1]

    P-47D 44-90471 (FAP114)
    P-47D 45-49181 (FAP115)
    P-47D 45-49167 (FAP116)
    P-47D 45-49192 (FAP119)
    P-47D 45-49205 (FAP122)
    P-47D 45-49335 (FAP127)

Perhaps the oldest Thunderbolt extant is P-47D (42-8068), a New Guinea veteran, variously reported in New Guinea and New Zealand. Next comes the razorback D-model (42-8205; U.S. registration N14519) in the collection of the Champlin Fighter Museum of Mesa, Arizona, as of this writing.

The razorback P-47D (42-23278) resurrected by Republic in 1961 for the 20th anniversary of the first flight of the Thunderbolt was damaged several years later, and passed into the collection of the Air Force Museum.[2]

An enduring presence at Ed Mal-

In 1961, this refurbished razorback P-47D helped Republic Aviation commemorate the type's 20th anniversary. (SDAM)

Spurious ETO markings and invasion stripes adorned a P-47N on permanent display at Lackland Air Force Base, San Antonio, Texas, when photographed in July 1994. (Frederick A. Johnsen)

Silver P-47D posed with a Republic F-105D Thunderchief during 20th anniversary ceremonies for the Thunderbolt. (USAFM)

oney's Planes of Fame Museum in Chino, California, is Curtiss-built P-47G 42-25234. This razorback Jug survived the war as an instructional airframe at the Cal-Aero Technical Institute in Glendale, California. Displayed at various times in static and airworthy condition, this P-47G sustained damage in a crash in 1971, subsequently undergoing rebuild at Chino. Another remarkable surviving G-model (42-25068; N42354, later N47DG) also escaped the postwar scrapper as a technical school airframe. It passed through surplus aircraft dealer Jack Hardwick's facility in El Monte, California, and ultimately emerged on the warbird scene in the mid-1980s as the masterfully restored aircraft of Ray Stutsman in Indiana, before moving to a new owner.

Foreign countries employing Thunderbolts had a penchant for keeping at least one example as a display. P-47s have been reported preserved in Brazil, Colombia, Cuba, France, England, Italy, Mexico, Turkey, Venezuela, and Yugoslavia. The highly-mobile world of warbirds has seen several Thunderbolts migrate to new ownership in other countries.

[1] John Chapman and Geoff Goodall, *Warbirds Worldwide Directory*, Warbirds Worldwide Ltd., Mansfield, England, 1989. [2] *Ibid.*

APPENDIX A

AMERICAN P-47 UNITS

P-47s roamed Europe, the Far East, and Pacific outposts like Ie Shima by war's end in 1945. A few survived into postwar years in American service, but saw no further combat as U.S. aircraft.

1st Air Commando Group: Operated P-47s in Burma circa May 1944 to May 1945, preceded and followed by P-51s.

4th Fighter Group: Converted to P-47s from Spitfires in March 1943, thence to P-51s in April 1944 as part of Eighth Air Force.

14th Fighter Group: Reactivated at Dow Field, Maine, on 20 November 1946 and initially equipped with P-47s at that time.

18th Fighter Group: Following illustrious wartime Pacific career with other fighter types, received F-47s in late 1947 before converting to F-51s and then F-80s by 1949.

21st Fighter Group: After Pacific wartime missions in P-39s, P-38s, and P-51s, gained P-47s in the summer of 1946; unit inactivated on Guam later that year.

23rd Fighter Group: After postwar inactivation, the group was activated on Guam on 10 October 1946 with P-47s; unit subsequently moved to the Panama Canal Zone where it was inactivated on 24 September 1949.

27th Fighter Group: Converted to P-47s in Mediterranean Theater in June 1944; inactivated on 7 November 1945; activated in Germany in August 1946 and equipped with P-47s for less than a year.

33rd Fighter Group: Trained with P-47s and P-38s in India in the spring of 1944; flew combat in China with 14th Air Force and India-Burma with 10th Air Force.

35th Fighter Group: Served in World War Two under Fifth Air Force; operated P-47s from late 1943 to March 1945.

36th Fighter Group: After flying P-39s and P-40s in support of the Panama Canal, the unit returned to the U.S. in mid-1943 to train with P-47s; sent to England under Ninth Air Force beginning May 1944; postwar iteration again based in Panama, with P-47s from about October 1946 until switching to F-80s by December 1947.

48th Fighter Group: Arrived in England in March 1944, for assignment to Ninth Air Force; trained with P-47s and made first combat mission on 20 April 1944. One unusual mission was air-dropping of blood plasma in belly tanks, to ground forces.

49th Fighter Group: Flew a variety of fighters in the New Guinea campaign, including some P-47s, until completely furnished with P-38s by September 1944.

50th Fighter Group: Included P-47s in its roster for testing and training in fighter operations; moved to England in the spring of 1944 under Ninth Air Force, and began P-47 combat operations on 1 May 1944.

51st Fighter Group: Postwar reactivation on Okinawa in October 1946 included use of P-47s and P-61s, moving into F-80s and F-82s by 1948.

53rd Fighter Group: Trained replacement pilots in Third Air Force in the U.S. on a variety of fighters including P-47s; unit disbanded 1 May 1944.

56th Fighter Group: Received P-47s in June 1942 and trained for combat; moved to England by January 1943. Flew early P-47 combat over Europe in April 1943. After inactivation in 1945, postwar reactivation included some P-47s and P-51s, based at Selfridge Field, Michigan, by mid-1946.

57th Fighter Group: Converted from P-40s to P-47s in early 1944; flew interdiction and other sorties in Italy and southern France.

58th Fighter Group: Trained with P-47s in 1943; flew operations in New Guinea campaign beginning in February 1944 as part of Fifth Air Force, moving to the Philippines and Okinawa.

78th Fighter Group: Following P-38 training, the group was re-equipped with P-47s and began operations from England under

Eighth Air Force in April 1943, converting by the end of 1944 to P-51s.

79th Fighter Group: In the MTO, during the push toward Rome, the group traded its Curtiss P-40s for P-47 Thunderbolts, which it used over Italy and Southern France as part of 12th Air Force.

80th Fighter Group: Used P-47s to train for combat, as well as providing defense for portions of the northeastern United States; moved to CBI under 10th Air Force in 1943, flying P-38s and P-40s, later gaining P-47s.

81st Fighter Group: Following MTO service with P-39s, the unit moved in the spring of 1944 to India and trained with P-47s and P-40s, thence to China and the 14th Air Force. Following postwar inactivation/activation cycle, acquired P-51s in 1946 in Hawaii, and then F-47s early in 1948.

83rd Fighter Group: Stateside P-47 replacement training unit at Richmond, Virginia, and then Dover, Delaware in part of 1943 and 1944; unit disbanded 10 April 1944.

84th Fighter Group: This stateside training unit included some P-47s in its complement in 1943-44.

85th Fighter Group: Received some P-47s in March 1944; unit disbanded on 1 May of that year. The group was a replacement training unit when it had P-47s.

86th Fighter Group: Included P-47s in its roster; flew combat over Sicily and on to Italy and southern France. Again used F-47s during a postwar stint in Europe.

87th Fighter Group: Used P-47s to train replacement pilots in First Air Force during part of 1943-44.

103rd Fighter-Interceptor Group: Flew F-47s in 1951 under Air Defense Command.

108th Fighter-Bomber Group: Postwar unit, assigned variously to Strategic Air Command and Tactical Air Command; flew F-47s circa 1951-52.

118th Tactical Reconnaissance Group: Used some RF-47s and other aircraft for training and maneuvers under Tactical Air Command circa 1951-52.

318th Fighter Group: Flew P-47s in Hawaii, and later the Marianas and Ryukyus.

324th Fighter Group: Picked up P-47s in July 1944 while fighting in the Italian campaign.

325th Fighter Group: Evolved from P-40s to P-47s, and then P-51s in the MTO.

326th Fighter Group: Trained replacement pilots in P-47s.

327th Fighter Group: Stateside air defense and training unit, flying P-47s from February 1943 until the unit disbanded on 10 April 1944.

332nd Fighter Group: Used P-47s briefly in April-May 1944 under 12th Air Force in the MTO; again received P-47s in 1947 during postwar activation.

338th Fighter Group: Third Air Force training unit; disbanded 1 May 1944.

348th Fighter Group: Flew P-47s in southwest Pacific, under Fifth Air Force, moving with the fighting to the Philippines by November 1944.

350th Fighter Group: Converted to P-47s August-September 1944 under 12th Air Force.

352nd Fighter Group: Performed U.S. air defense while training for overseas duty with P-47s, late 1942 into 1943; began combat from England in September 1943. Converted to P-51s in April 1944.

353rd Fighter Group: Began flying combat from England in P-47s in August 1943; converted to P-51s in October 1944.

354th Fighter Group: Flew P-47s from November 1944 to February 1945; flew P-51s before and after this time.

355th Fighter Group: Flew combat from England beginning in September 1943; converted to P-51s circa March-April 1944.

356th Fighter Group: Starting in October 1943, flew combat under Eighth Air Force; converted to P-51s from P-47s in November 1944.

358th Fighter Group: Began combat in December 1943 with P-47s in Eighth, and later Ninth, Air Forces.

359th Fighter Group: Began combat as an Eighth Air Force P-47 unit in December 1943; converted to P-51s by April 1944.

361st Fighter Group: Entered combat from England on 21 January 1944; converted to P-51s by May of that year.

362nd Fighter Group: Ninth Air Force unit; flew first combat on 8 February 1944, escorting B-24s.

365th Fighter Group: Trained with P-47s, moving to England in December 1943. Started flying combat in February 1944 under Ninth Air Force.

366th Fighter Group: Ninth Air Force unit, entering combat with P-47s on 14 March 1944 in a fighter sweep along the French coastline.

367th Fighter Group: Converted from P-38s to P-47s in February 1945; assigned to Ninth Air Force.

368th Fighter Group: Began combat on 14 March 1944 with P-47s, in Ninth Air Force.

370th Fighter Group: Ninth Air Force unit; trained in P-47s, but entered combat in P-38s in May 1944.

371st Fighter Group: Began Ninth Air Force operations in P-47s in April 1944.

373rd Fighter Group: Trained for combat in P-47s; moved to England and first flew combat on 8 May 1944 in a fighter sweep over Normandy, as part of Ninth Air Force.

402nd Fighter Group: Trained P-47 replacement pilots in late 1943 and early 1944, as part of First Air Force.

404th Fighter Group: Also designated 404th Fighter-Bomber Group between August 1943 and May 1944; trained in P-47s, P-39s, and other aircraft; moved to England, and Ninth Air Force. Flew first combat in P-47s in May 1944.

405th Fighter Group: Trained in a variety of aircraft including P-47s; entered combat under Ninth Air Force with P-47s in April 1944.

406th Fighter Group: Trained on a variety of aircraft including P-47s; moved to England under Ninth Air Force in April 1944 and began combat in P-47s the following month.

407th Fighter-Bomber Group: While serving as a replacement training unit, included P-47s in its repertoire, circa late 1943-early 1944.

408th Fighter-Bomber Group: Included P-47s for stateside training in part of 1943 and 1944.

413th Fighter Group: Began training in P-47s for long-range operations in October 1944; served from bases in Saipan and later Ie Shima, mostly on ground-attack sorties, including targets in Japan.

414th Fighter Group: Took P-47s to the Pacific in the summer of 1945 in time for combat against Japan.

477th Composite Group: Assigned to First Air Force with P-47s and B-25s in 1945 for stateside use.

507th Fighter Group: Assigned to 20th Air Force in the Pacific in mid-1945 and to Eighth Air Force, also then in the Pacific, by August 1945; flew combat out of Ie Shima in P-47s from 1 July 1945.

508th Fighter Group: Moved to Hawaii in January 1945 after training with P-47s; supported defense of Hawaii, trained replacement pilots, and repaired P-47s and P-51s from other units. Unit inactivated in Hawaii on 25 November 1945.

Air National Guard Thunderbolt Squadrons:

101st (Massachusetts);
104th (Maryland);
105th (Tennessee);
118th (Connecticut);
119th (New Jersey);
121st (District of Columbia);
128th (Georgia);
131st (Massachusetts);
132nd (Maine);
133rd (New Hampshire);
134th (Vermont);
136th (New York);
137th (New York);
138th (New York);
139th (New York);
141st (New Jersey);
142nd (Delaware);
146th (Pennsylvania);
147th (Pennsylvania);
148th (Pennsylvania);
149th (Virginia);
152nd (Rhode Island);
153rd (Mississippi);
156th (North Carolina);
158th (Georgia);
167th (West Virginia);
198th (Puerto Rico); and
199th (Hawaii).

(See also: *Air Force Combat Units of World War II,* by Maurer Maurer, and *The Air Guard,* by Rene Francillon)

Significant Dates

Key Dates in the History of the P-47 Thunderbolt

6 September 1940: Lightweight XP-47 contract modified to allow the heavy XP-47B to be built instead.

6 May 1941: First flight of the XP-47B.

December 1941: Delivery of first production P-47B.

8 August 1942: Prototype XP-47B demolished in crash before testing was finished.

September 1942: Last P-47B completed; First P-47C delivered.

September 1942: XP-47E, a pressurized-cockpit conversion of a P-47B, completed.

December 1942: First Curtiss contract-built P-47G delivered; Curtiss P-47G production ended after 354 G-models were delivered by March 1944.

8 April 1943: P-47 combat debut, as Eighth Air Force squadrons took C-models over the Continent.

15 April 1943: First P-47 victory made over Europe, by Fourth Fighter Group.

June 1943: First P-47s in Fifth Air Force, assigned to the 348th Fighter Group, arrived at Port Moresby to fight the Japanese.

The P-47 turbosupercharger access door was held in place by eight fasteners, as seen on an example at Strother Field, Kansas. (AFHRA)

3 July 1943: Bubble canopy conversion completed as XP-47K.

March 1944: Completion of Curtiss P-47G contract.

April 1944: Both Republic P-47 assembly lines switched to building bubble-top D-models instead of razorbacks.

20 July 1944: Lt. Col. Francis Gabreski, Thunderbolt ace with 28 victories, crash-landed near Bassinheim airfield, and subsequently captured by Germans and imprisoned in Stalag Luft I.

5 August 1944: Republic claimed a top speed of 505 miles an hour for the XP-47J. Army Air Forces tests in 1945 could only verify a computed speed of 493 miles per hour at 35,000 feet — still no mean feat.

September 1944: Royal Air Force Thunderbolts commenced operations over Burma.

October 1944: Brazilian P-47 squadron flew in Italy.

25 May 1945: 318th Fighter Group destroyed 34 Japanese airplanes without sustaining any losses.

26 July 1945: First flight of XP-47H, with Chrysler XIV-2220-1 engine.

December 1945: Production ended with delivery of the last Thunderbolt, a P-47N from the Farmingdale assembly line.

1954: Last F-47s in U.S. Air National Guard service replaced.

June 1954: Thunderbolts saw combat action during revolution in Guatemala.